Hong Kong

Cultural Awareness and Business Negotiations

Country Study

Contents

INTRODUCTION

In our increasingly interconnected world, understanding and embracing cultural diversity has become essential for both personal and professional success. This series of Cultural Awareness books aims to provide participants with the knowledge, skills, and tools necessary to better understand and navigate various cultural contexts. By investing in cultural awareness, we are not only fostering stronger relationships but also paving the way for more successful business ventures and personal growth.

The expanding Global market presents immense opportunities for businesses. However, these opportunities come with the responsibility of understanding the nuances of various cultures. Unintentional cultural misunderstandings can jeopardise your chances of securing a crucial foothold in this lucrative market. This series highlights the importance of being aware of cultural differences and equips you with the tools to deal with the challenges that may arise when interacting with individuals from different cultural backgrounds.

Individuals and families who have travelled or are planning to move to different countries also face the challenge of adapting to new cultures. Culture shock can be overwhelming if one is not prepared to handle the changes that come with relocating. This course offers practical insights and tools to help individuals and families better understand and navigate the complexities of their new cultural environment.

Cultural awareness goes beyond learning facts or memorizing customs; it is about cultivating a genuine appreciation for the richness of human experiences. This series encourages participants to look beyond their own cultural lens and develop empathy for the perspectives of others. By doing so, we foster a more inclusive and harmonious world where people from diverse backgrounds can come together and create meaningful connections.

Throughout this book, you will be introduced to various cultural frameworks, practices, and traditions, as well as common misconceptions and stereotypes that often contribute to misunderstandings and miscommunications. Engaging with these topics will enable you to recognise cultural differences, appreciate their value, and navigate them effectively.

In conclusion, cultural awareness is essential for anyone aiming to expand their reach in the global market, adapt to new cultural environments, or enrich their lives by embracing the beauty of human diversity. By undertaking this journey, you are taking a significant step toward creating a more inclusive, empathetic, and successful future.

Ask yourself: Can you afford to miss out on the vital opportunities and personal growth that cultural awareness can bring to your life? The time to invest in cultural understanding is now. Welcome to an enlightening and transformative journey.

1. WHAT IS CULTURE?

What is Culture?

The Culture of a people can be understood as the system of shared ideas and meanings, explicit and implicit, which a people use to interpret the world, and which serve to pattern their behaviour.

This includes an understanding of the art, literature, and history of a society, but also less tangible aspects such as attitudes, prejudices, folklore etc. Unconscious or conscious habits are just as important as art and history.

Values - What people say one ought to do or not do? What is considered good or bad - the importance of honesty, or chastity?

Laws - What political authorities have decided people should do, and what the sanctions are?

Rules - What a society has decided its members should do. Social rules about marriage ages, childrearing.

Social Categories- Ways of thinking about people as types. - "friends", "criminals", "lovers", "nobles", "clergy".

Tacit Models - Implicit standards and patterns of behaviour that a person does not think about - knowing how to address a police officer rather than friends. Knowing how to dress for a job interview as opposed to a dance.

Fundamental - Categories and ways of thinking that people take for granted and may not recognise even when pointed out. - thinking in dualities good/bad, male/female.

Culture shapes

- The way we think
- The way we interact
- The way we communicate
- The way we transmit knowledge to the next generation

Culture manifests itself in

- Food
- Religion
- Dress
- Differences in language
- Our expectations of male and female roles
- Non-verbal rules and body language

The first step is in understanding the values and rules for behaviour of our own culture - the "normal" or "right" way of doing things. What makes us different?

Geert Hofstede

Between 1967 and 1973 Geert Hofstede conducted a study on culture across 100 000 employees of IBM in 50 countries. From this he developed a framework to 'measure' the 'value dimensions' of various cultures.

Hofstede identified 4 values which can be related to each culture:

- Individualism
- Masculinity
- Power Distance, and
- Uncertainty Avoidance

Later studies by Trompenaar have added several more; however, I will address the 4 basic values along with one later addition relating to time.

From surveys, Hofstede was able to map the cultures and compare them, and from this extrapolate as to why a culture may act in a particular way.

Taking the basic values separately, measured on a scale of 0 to 100;

	PD	ID	M	UA	LT
HK	68H	25L	57M	29L	17L
AUS	38L	90H	61H	51M	21L
USA	40	91	62	46	26
UK	35	89	66	35	51

H = top third of countries

M = medium

L = bottom third

Power Distance

In this dimension, we explore the concept that not all individuals within societies are equal, reflecting the culture's attitude towards these disparities. Power Distance is defined as the degree to which less powerful members of institutions and organizations within a country anticipate and accept that power is distributed unevenly.

With a score of **68**, Hong Kong exhibits a significant degree of Power Distance Index, reflecting a society that accepts inequalities among its members. In this environment, the relationships between subordinates and superiors can be quite distinct, and there may be limited safeguards against the misuse of power by those in higher positions. Individuals tend to be swayed by official authority and repercussions, while generally maintaining a positive outlook on people's abilities to lead and take initiative.

Individualism v. Collectivism

This dimension addresses the level of interdependence that a society maintains among its members, focusing on whether individuals perceive themselves in terms of "I" or "We." In individualistic societies, people are expected to take care of themselves and their immediate family members only. In collectivist societies, individuals belong to 'in-groups' (such as families, clans, or organizations) that provide care and support in exchange for loyalty.

With a score of **25**, Hong Kong exhibits a collectivist culture where individuals prioritize the interests of their group over their own. In-group considerations influence hiring and promotion decisions, with closer in-groups (such as family) often receiving preferential treatment. While relationships among in-group members tend to be cooperative, interactions with out-groups can be cold or even hostile. Personal connections take precedence over tasks and company objectives. Communication tends to be indirect, as maintaining group harmony is crucial and open conflicts are generally avoided.

Masculinity v. Femininity

A high score (Masculine) on this dimension signifies that a society is driven by competition, achievement, and success, where success is defined by being the winner or the best in one's field. This value system starts in school and continues throughout organizational life.

A low score (Feminine) on this dimension indicates that the dominant values in society prioritize caring for others and quality of life. In a Feminine society, quality of life is considered a sign of success, and standing out from the crowd is not admired. The fundamental issue here is what motivates people: wanting to be the best (Masculine) or enjoying what they do (Feminine).

With a score of **57**, Hong Kong exhibits a moderately masculine society, characterized by a focus on success and ambition. The drive for achievement is evident in the long hours many individuals spend at work. Service providers, such as hairdressers, often offer services well into the night. Another example of this success-oriented mindset is the significant emphasis students place on their exam scores and rankings, as these factors are crucial in determining their future success.

In feminine countries, the focus is on "working to live," where managers seek consensus, and people prioritize equality, solidarity, and quality in their work lives. Conflicts are resolved through compromise and negotiation; with incentives such as free time and flexibility being favoured. The emphasis is on well-being, and status is not flaunted. An effective manager is a supportive one, and decision-making involves participation. In contrast, low masculine countries, which are not feminine enough to be classified as feminine societies, exhibit masculine traits but to a lesser degree.

Uncertainty Avoidance

The Uncertainty Avoidance dimension addresses how societies cope with the fact that the future is always uncertain: should we attempt to control the future or simply let it unfold? The inherent ambiguity in the future creates anxiety, and different cultures have developed various ways to manage this anxiety. The extent to which a culture's members feel threatened by ambiguous or unknown situations and have established beliefs and institutions to mitigate these uncertainties is reflected in their Uncertainty Avoidance score.

With a notably low score of **29**, Hong Kong displays a low level of Uncertainty Avoidance. Flexibility in adhering to laws and rules is often exercised to accommodate specific situations, and pragmatism is a prevailing attitude. Hong Kong residents are at ease with ambiguity, as demonstrated by the Chinese language, which is rich in nuanced meanings that can be challenging for Westerners to grasp. This adaptability contributes to their entrepreneurial spirit.

Long Term Orientation

With a significant score of **61**, Hong Kong's culture is decidedly pragmatic. In such societies, individuals understand that truth is often contingent on the situation, context, and time. They demonstrate a capacity to adapt traditions to changing conditions with ease, exhibit a strong inclination to save and invest, practice thriftiness, and display perseverance in achieving their goals.

Acculturation

Acculturation is the process of adapting to a new culture.

- Variables affecting Acculturation
- The amount of time spent in the process – educating yourself
- The quantity and quality of interaction – trying things
- Ethnicity or nation of origin – how far is it removed from our own
- Affinity – willingness to learn and adapt

Stages of Acculturation

- Acceptance of new culture - honeymoon
- Individual starts to feel comfortable in the new culture
- Feelings of anger, hostility, and frustration
- Recovery
- Culture Shock

Generalisations

We should remember that there will probably never be one person within a culture that actually meets these dimensions. Rather this is a tool to anticipate likely reaction of a particular culture. There is never an average person! What should be remembered is that between the extremes, patterns do exist.

The inverse also applies; do not confuse a particular individual's personality as representative of culture. Whilst Australian's are considered sports loving people, there are people who don't like Rugby – as hard as that is to believe!

Stereotyping – setting a standard idea, concept or form. This 'notion' has a deeper meaning to our basic survival instincts.

Bias – a particular tendency or preference, which may prevent unprejudiced consideration of a topic. A 'learned' response.

Prejudice - an unfavourable opinion formed beforehand or without knowledge or reason.

Linear and Circular Thinking

How does culture affect Management?

Our Western (Greek) method of teaching & learning is if there is a problem then I can solve it. We are taught to identify issues as a 'problem' that challenges us. The individual works out a plan and overcomes the problem.

In a culture not rooted in the Western traditions, the issue may not be seen as a 'problem'!! Rather it is a divergence or even a side issue that can be avoided or not confronted until a solution is evident

Managing Across Culture

The management theory of MBI (Mapping – Bridging – Integrating) was developed to understand the differences and work out optimum paths to achieve greater workflows.

2. INTRODUCTION

The Importance of Cultural Awareness for Families and Business

In today's increasingly interconnected world, understanding and embracing different cultures is essential for both personal and professional success. With the advent of globalization and the ease of international travel, families and businesses alike find themselves navigating new cultural landscapes. For those moving to or conducting business in another country, cultivating cultural awareness is crucial to ensure a smooth transition and build lasting relationships in this vibrant country.

For families relocating, cultural awareness is the key to integrating successfully into their new home. By understanding the customs, values, and social norms of a society, families can better adapt to their surroundings and foster meaningful connections with their new neighbours. Familiarizing oneself with the language, local etiquette, and traditions can help ease the challenges of adjusting to a new environment, allowing families to fully immerse themselves in the rich cultural tapestry of a new country.

In the realm of business, cultural awareness is equally important. As countries continue to grow as economic powers, many international companies and entrepreneurs are seizing opportunities in the dynamic markets. Mastering the intricacies of business culture can help professionals negotiate deals effectively, avoid misunderstandings, and forge strong partnerships with their counterparts. By respecting local customs and demonstrating cultural sensitivity, businesspeople can build trust and credibility, essential ingredients for success in any international venture.

This comprehensive guide aims to equip families and professionals with the knowledge and tools necessary to embrace a foreign culture and thrive in their personal and professional lives. Through an exploration of history, values, and social norms, readers will gain valuable insights into the intricacies of a society. Additionally, practical advice on navigating daily life, social interactions, and business negotiations will empower families and professionals alike to make the most of their time in this captivating country.

As you embark on your journey, remember that cultural awareness is an ongoing process, requiring patience, openness, and a willingness to learn. By embracing the unique qualities that make a different culture such a fascinating place to live and work, you can create lasting memories, foster meaningful relationships, and unlock the full potential of your experience in this remarkable country.

The Importance of Understanding Culture in Hong Kong

Hong Kong, a vibrant city known for its rich history, diverse population, and unique blend of Eastern and Western influences, offers a fascinating cultural experience. As a global business hub and a popular tourist destination, it is essential to understand the importance of culture in Hong Kong to foster effective communication, collaboration, and mutual respect among its residents and visitors.

Business Etiquette and Practices

In a city renowned for its international business prowess, understanding Hong Kong's cultural nuances can significantly impact the success of business dealings. The city's business etiquette is deeply rooted in its collectivist culture, emphasizing the importance of personal relationships and group harmony. Building trust and cultivating connections are vital for successful business negotiations. Awareness of these cultural factors can help foreign companies and professionals navigate the local business landscape more effectively and avoid potential misunderstandings that could jeopardize business relationships.

Communication Styles

Hong Kong's communication style is typically indirect, emphasizing politeness and respect for hierarchy. The Chinese language, with its abundance of nuanced meanings, reflects this tendency towards ambiguity. To maintain harmonious relationships and avoid conflicts, it is crucial for foreigners to recognize and adapt to this communication style. This might involve paying attention to nonverbal cues, interpreting messages carefully, and seeking clarification when necessary to ensure that the intended meaning is accurately conveyed.

Social Customs and Traditions

Hong Kong's diverse cultural heritage is evident in its wide range of customs, traditions, and festivals. Understanding these practices is essential for fostering cultural sensitivity and appreciation. For instance, the Chinese New Year, Dragon Boat Festival, and Mid-Autumn Festival are significant events in Hong Kong, each with their unique customs and significance. Participating in or acknowledging these festivities can help foreigners develop stronger connections with locals and demonstrate respect for their traditions.

Adapting to the Local Lifestyle

Hong Kong's low Uncertainty Avoidance score reflects the city's adaptability and entrepreneurial spirit. As a result, locals tend to be more comfortable with ambiguity and change than those from other cultures. By understanding and embracing this aspect of Hong

Kong's culture, foreigners can better adapt to the local lifestyle, develop a sense of belonging, and appreciate the city's dynamic nature.

Dining Etiquette

Hong Kong is famous for its culinary scene, offering a diverse array of local and international cuisines. However, it is essential to be aware of the city's dining etiquette to enjoy a harmonious dining experience. For example, it is customary to use chopsticks and share dishes in a family-style setting. Additionally, it is considered polite to wait for the host or the most senior person at the table to start eating before joining in. Understanding these customs can help visitors feel more comfortable and accepted in social situations.

Multiculturalism and Inclusivity

Hong Kong's multiculturalism is one of its most appealing aspects. With people from various backgrounds and nationalities residing in the city, understanding and embracing diverse cultures is critical for promoting inclusivity and mutual respect. By fostering an environment that celebrates diversity, Hong Kong continues to thrive as a global metropolis.

3. UNDERSTANDING CULTURE IN HONG KONG

A Brief History of Hong Kong

Hong Kong, a Special Administrative Region of China, has a rich and complex history. Its unique blend of Eastern and Western influences can be traced back to various historical events that have shaped the city over the years.

Early History

Archaeological findings suggest Hong Kong has been inhabited since the Old Stone Age, around 30,000 years ago. The rich history of human presence in the region can be traced back to the Palaeolithic Era, as evidenced by the discovery of stone tools and pottery shards at various archaeological sites. Early inhabitants were likely hunter-gatherers who roamed the area in search of food, water, and shelter.

During the **Han Dynasty** (206 BC - 220 AD), the region that is now Hong Kong was incorporated into the Chinese Empire. The Han rulers sought to extend their influence southward and establish control over the various tribes and kingdoms that inhabited the region. The Han administration developed a sophisticated system of governance, which included the establishment of counties and the appointment of local officials to oversee and manage the population.

Throughout the **Tang** (618-907 AD) and **Song** (960-1279 AD) Dynasties, Hong Kong served as a vital coastal trading and military outpost. Its strategic location on the southern coast of China made it an essential hub for maritime trade and communication between the Chinese mainland, Southeast Asia, and the Indian Ocean. The thriving trade in the region attracted merchants from near and far, who sought to capitalize on the abundant resources and market opportunities available.

The Tang and Song Dynasties saw a significant increase in the population of Hong Kong, which led to the growth of urban settlements and the establishment of various industries, such as pottery making, shipbuilding, and salt production. The region also witnessed significant advancements in technology, agriculture, and the arts, as trade and cultural exchanges facilitated the dissemination of knowledge and ideas.

During the **Mongol invasion of China** in the late 13th century, Hong Kong played a crucial role as a defensive stronghold. It provided a base for the Southern Song Dynasty's naval forces to resist the invading Mongol armies. Despite its strategic importance, the region eventually fell under Mongol rule, and Hong Kong became part of the vast Mongol Empire under the **Yuan Dynasty** (1271-1368 AD).

The decline of the Mongol Empire led to the rise of the Ming Dynasty (1368-1644 AD) in China, which sought to re-establish Chinese control over the region. Hong Kong continued to play a significant role in the Ming Dynasty's maritime trade network, connecting China with the rest of the world. The Ming rulers also sought to strengthen the region's defences by constructing military installations, such as watchtowers and beacon towers, to guard against potential threats from the sea.

The Ming and Qing Dynasties

During the **Ming** (1368-1644 AD) and **Qing** (1644-1911 AD) Dynasties, Hong Kong's strategic coastal location attracted merchants and fishermen, who established small settlements in the area. These settlements eventually grew into thriving communities that were primarily dependent on fishing, agriculture, and maritime trade for their livelihoods.

During the Ming Dynasty, the Chinese government actively encouraged maritime trade and exploration, which led to a significant increase in commercial activities along the southern coast of China. Hong Kong emerged as an important centre for maritime trade, serving as a vital link between the Chinese mainland and the flourishing markets of Southeast Asia, India, the Middle East, and even Europe. Chinese merchants, as well as traders from other countries, flocked to the region to take advantage of the lucrative trade opportunities.

The burgeoning maritime trade in the region also attracted pirates who sought to profit from the wealth of the merchants and the trade routes. Hong Kong's sheltered harbors, numerous islands, and complex coastline provided ideal hiding places for pirate ships, allowing them to easily launch surprise attacks on unsuspecting trading vessels. During the latter part of the Ming Dynasty, piracy became a significant problem in the South China Sea, and Hong Kong's waters were no exception.

The rise of piracy in the region can be partly attributed to the socio-political turmoil that plagued the late Ming Dynasty. Corruption, economic hardships, and political infighting weakened the central government's ability to effectively deal with the pirate threat. Many pirates were former soldiers or sailors who had fallen on hard times, and some even gained the support of local officials, further complicating efforts to eradicate piracy.

The situation worsened during the transition from the Ming to the Qing Dynasty, as many pirate groups took advantage of the power vacuum to expand their operations. The most famous pirate of this era was the legendary **Zheng Chenggong**, also known as Koxinga, who established a formidable pirate fleet and even managed to capture the island of Taiwan from the Dutch in 1662.

The Qing Dynasty, which succeeded the Ming, adopted a more stringent approach to dealing with piracy. They implemented the "Sea Ban" policy, which severely restricted maritime trade and movement along the coast in an effort to cut off resources and support for the pirates. This policy, however, had the unintended consequence of crippling the coastal economy, leading many fishermen and traders to turn to piracy as a means of survival.

As the Qing Dynasty consolidated its power and gradually lifted the **Sea Ban policy**, maritime trade began to flourish once again in the South China Sea, and Hong Kong's importance as a trade hub grew. The Qing government also increased its efforts to suppress piracy, deploying naval forces to patrol the waters and offering amnesty to pirates who agreed to surrender and join the imperial navy.

Despite these efforts, piracy remained a constant challenge for the Qing authorities, as new pirate groups emerged to replace those that had been defeated or disbanded. In the early 19th century, the infamous pirate queen **Ching Shih** commanded a formidable fleet that terrorized the waters around Hong Kong and southern China. Ultimately, it was only through a combination of diplomacy, military force, and economic incentives that the Qing Dynasty was able to significantly reduce the pirate threat in the region.

The Opium Wars and British Colonization

The **First Opium War** (1839-1842) between China and Britain marked a turning point in the history of Hong Kong. The conflict had its roots in the longstanding trade imbalances between the two nations, particularly the British sale of **opium** to China. The **British East India Company** had been importing large quantities of tea, silk, and porcelain from China, but China had little interest in British goods, leading to a trade deficit. To bridge the gap, Britain began exporting opium, which they sourced from India to China.

The widespread use of opium led to severe social and economic problems in China, including widespread addiction and a massive outflow of silver. In response, the Chinese government imposed a ban on opium imports and confiscated and destroyed large quantities of the drug. This move led to a series of diplomatic confrontations and ultimately escalated into armed conflict between the two nations.

The First Opium War saw a series of decisive naval and land engagements that demonstrated the technological and military superiority of the British forces. The Chinese were ill-equipped to face the modern firepower and tactics of the British, and their defeat was inevitable. The conflict concluded with the **Treaty of Nanking**, signed in 1842, which forced China to cede Hong Kong Island to the British, along with other concessions.

The British established Hong Kong as a free port, attracting traders from around the world. The region's strategic location, deep-water harbor, and status as a free port made it an ideal base for international trade and commerce. Hong Kong soon became a thriving trade hub, with merchants from Europe, America, and other parts of Asia flocking to the city to take advantage of the economic opportunities it offered.

Following the **Second Opium War** (1856-1860), which further exposed the weaknesses of the Chinese government and military, the **Kowloon Peninsula** was also ceded to Britain under the **Convention of Beijing** in 1860. This territorial expansion provided the British with additional land for development and helped secure the harbor from potential threats.

In 1898, with the expiration of the lease on the **New Territories** approaching, the British sought to further expand their territory in Hong Kong. They negotiated the **Second Convention of Peking**, which granted them a 99-year lease on the New Territories, significantly increasing the size of their colonial holdings in the region.

The British administration transformed Hong Kong into a modern, cosmopolitan city, investing heavily in infrastructure and public services. The development of the region was characterized by the construction of roads, railways, and public buildings, as well as the establishment of a legal system, police force, and educational institutions.

Under British rule, Hong Kong experienced rapid economic growth and became a crucial financial and trading centre in Asia. The city's population also grew exponentially, as people from mainland China and other parts of the world were drawn to the economic opportunities and relative stability it offered.

Japanese Occupation

During World War II, Hong Kong found itself in the midst of the turmoil that had engulfed the Asia-Pacific region. The city was occupied by Japanese forces from 1941 to 1945, following a brief but intense period of fighting known as the Battle of Hong Kong. The British, who were already grappling with the war in Europe, were unable to mount a successful defence against the Japanese invasion.

The **Japanese occupation** had a profound impact on Hong Kong and its people. The city's population declined drastically during this time, with estimates suggesting that the number of residents fell from approximately 1.6 million in 1941 to around 600,000 in 1945. This dramatic decrease resulted from a combination of factors, including forced deportations, migration to mainland China, and the severe hardships endured by the population under Japanese rule.

Hong Kong's economy also suffered significant damage during the occupation. The Japanese authorities imposed a harsh regime of control and exploitation, commandeering resources and infrastructure for their own purposes. Hong Kong's once-thriving trade and financial sectors were crippled, as the city's status as a free port was suspended, and many businesses were either closed or taken over by the Japanese.

The city's infrastructure, which had been developed extensively under British rule, was left in a state of disrepair by the end of the occupation. The extensive damage to roads, railways, and utilities, as well as the widespread destruction of public buildings and private property, further hampered Hong Kong's recovery in the immediate aftermath of the war.

The British resumed control of Hong Kong after Japan's surrender in 1945, but the city they returned to was a far cry from the bustling metropolis it had been before the war. Faced with the enormous task of rebuilding, the British administration embarked on an ambitious program of reconstruction and development aimed at restoring Hong Kong's infrastructure, economy, and social fabric.

One of the key challenges facing the British in the post-war period was addressing the massive influx of refugees from mainland China, who were fleeing the civil war between the Nationalists and the Communists. Hong Kong's population swelled dramatically in the late 1940s and early 1950s, putting immense strain on the city's resources and housing. To cope with this, the government initiated large-scale public housing projects, which provided affordable accommodation for thousands of families.

Post-War Developments

In the aftermath of World War II, Hong Kong underwent a period of rapid industrialization, transforming from a trading port into a manufacturing hub. This economic metamorphosis was driven by a confluence of factors, including the city's strategic location, favourable business environment, and the influx of skilled labour and entrepreneurs from mainland China.

The post-war years saw waves of immigrants arriving in Hong Kong from mainland China, particularly during the **Chinese Civil War** (1945-1949) and the **Cultural Revolution** (1966-1976). Many of these immigrants were fleeing political instability, violence, and economic hardship. They brought with them a wealth of expertise and entrepreneurial spirit, which contributed to the development of Hong Kong's burgeoning manufacturing sector.

The city's industrial growth was primarily cantered around the production of textiles, electronics, plastics, and other consumer goods. Hong Kong became an export-oriented economy, with its products finding markets across the globe. The local manufacturing sector was characterized by its adaptability, efficiency, and focus on quality, which helped Hong Kong's products compete successfully on the international stage.

This period of rapid industrialization and economic growth earned Hong Kong a place among the "**Four Asian Tigers**" – a group that also included South Korea, Taiwan, and Singapore. These economies were characterized by their exceptional growth rates, export-driven industrialization, and rapid development of modern infrastructure.

Several factors contributed to Hong Kong's economic success during this period. The city's status as a free port, with no tariffs or trade barriers, facilitated the smooth flow of goods and attracted foreign investment. The British colonial administration implemented a series of economic reforms that fostered a business-friendly environment, promoting competition and innovation. These policies included low corporate taxes, minimal government intervention in the economy, and strong protection of property rights.

The influx of immigrants from mainland China not only provided Hong Kong with a skilled and motivated workforce but also led to significant population growth. This population boom placed immense pressure on the city's housing and social infrastructure. In response, the colonial government embarked on large-scale public housing projects to accommodate the growing population. These housing estates, which offered affordable and hygienic living conditions, became a distinctive feature of Hong Kong's urban landscape.

Hong Kong's rapid economic growth also led to the development of modern infrastructure and public services. The colonial administration invested in the construction of roads, railways, ports, and utilities, which facilitated the movement of goods and people and contributed to the city's economic expansion. Additionally, the government supported the development of education and healthcare systems, which helped create a skilled and healthy workforce.

The industrial boom also had its challenges, including income inequality, labour disputes, and environmental pollution. However, the overall benefits of Hong Kong's economic transformation far outweighed its drawbacks. The city's rapid development lifted millions out of poverty and elevated Hong Kong to the status of a global economic powerhouse.

The 1984 Sino-British Joint Declaration

As the 99-year lease of the New Territories approached its end, Britain and China negotiated Hong Kong's future. The 1984 **Sino-British Joint Declaration** was a pivotal moment in Hong Kong's history, as it determined the framework for the city's future after the expiration of the British lease on the New Territories in 1997. The Joint Declaration, signed by the governments of the United Kingdom and the People's Republic of China on December 19, 1984, established the principles under which Hong Kong would be governed after its return to Chinese sovereignty.

The Joint Declaration consisted of eight sections and three annexes, which laid out the terms of Hong Kong's handover and its post-handover governance. The key points of the agreement were as follows:

- China would resume the exercise of sovereignty over Hong Kong, including Hong Kong Island, the Kowloon Peninsula, and the New Territories, with effect from July 1, 1997.
- Hong Kong would become a **Special Administrative Region** (SAR) of the People's Republic of China, maintaining a high degree of autonomy except in matters of foreign affairs and defence.
- The current social, economic, and legal systems in Hong Kong would remain unchanged for 50 years after the handover, ensuring continuity and stability.

- Hong Kong would continue to function as a separate customs territory, maintaining its status as a free port and an international financial centre.
- The SAR would have its own currency, the Hong Kong dollar, which would continue to be freely convertible.
- Hong Kong residents would enjoy the rights and freedoms enshrined in the International Covenant on Civil and Political Rights, the International Covenant on Economic, Social and Cultural Rights, and other international human rights instruments.
- The SAR would maintain its own police force, independent of the mainland's public security authorities.
- The chief executive of the SAR would be selected by election or through consultations held locally and appointed by the Central People's Government of China.

The signing of the Sino-British Joint Declaration marked the beginning of a transitional period for Hong Kong. Both the British and Chinese governments worked closely to prepare for the handover, establishing the framework for the smooth transfer of power and the preservation of Hong Kong's unique characteristics. This included drafting the **Basic Law of the Hong Kong SAR**, which would serve as the city's post-handover constitution.

The Joint Declaration and the "one country, two systems" principle it enshrined were seen as ground-breaking diplomatic achievements. They allowed Hong Kong to maintain its distinct economic, legal, and political systems within the context of Chinese sovereignty. This innovative arrangement was seen as a way to protect Hong Kong's way of life and to ensure the city's continued success as an international financial and trading hub.

However, the Joint Declaration has not been without its challenges. Since the handover in 1997, there have been concerns regarding the preservation of Hong Kong's autonomy and the protection of its residents' rights and freedoms. Tensions have arisen over issues such as electoral reform, freedom of speech, and the influence of mainland China on Hong Kong's affairs.

Return to China and Recent Developments

On July 1, 1997, Hong Kong officially became a Special Administrative Region (SAR) of China, marking the end of 156 years of British colonial rule. The handover was carried out under the framework of the 1984 Sino-British Joint Declaration and the "one country, two systems" principle, which sought to preserve Hong Kong's unique political, economic, and legal systems within the context of Chinese sovereignty.

Initially, the transition appeared to be smooth, with Hong Kong maintaining its status as an international financial and trading hub. The city continued to enjoy a high degree of autonomy, as well as the rights and freedoms enshrined in the Basic Law, the SAR's mini-constitution.

However, over the years, tensions between Hong Kong and mainland China have grown, fuelled by concerns over the erosion of the city's autonomy and the influence of the Chinese government on Hong Kong's affairs. These tensions have manifested in various forms, including large-scale protests, political controversies, and debates over the city's identity.

One of the key issues contributing to the growing tensions has been the question of democratic reform. The Basic Law stipulates that the ultimate aim is the selection of the Chief Executive and the Legislative Council by universal suffrage. However, progress toward this goal has been slow and contentious, with many Hong Kong residents feeling that Beijing has been exerting undue influence on the city's electoral processes. In 2014, the so-called Umbrella Movement saw thousands of people take to the streets to demand greater democracy and genuine universal suffrage. The protests, which lasted for several months, highlighted the deepening divide between Hong Kong and mainland China.

Another area of concern has been press freedom and freedom of speech. Hong Kong has historically enjoyed a vibrant and independent press, with media outlets operating free from the censorship that characterizes mainland China. However, in recent years, there have been growing fears that this independence is being compromised, as incidents of self-censorship, the dismissal of outspoken journalists, and the acquisition of media companies by mainland Chinese entities have raised alarm bells.

The influence of the Chinese government in Hong Kong's affairs has also become a contentious issue. Critics argue that Beijing has been encroaching on the city's autonomy, undermining the "one country, two systems" principle. This has been evidenced by cases such as the 2015 disappearance of booksellers who sold politically sensitive materials, and the disqualification of pro-democracy lawmakers from the Legislative Council.

These tensions have culminated in the massive 2019 anti-extradition bill protests, which were sparked by a proposed law that would have allowed criminal suspects to be extradited to mainland China. While the bill was eventually withdrawn, the protests evolved into a broader pro-democracy movement, highlighting the deep-rooted concerns of Hong Kong residents over their rights, freedoms, and autonomy.

Religion, Values, and Social Norms

Religion, values, and social norms play a significant role in shaping the cultural landscape and social fabric of any society. In the case of Hong Kong, the city's unique history, diverse population, and dynamic cultural influences have resulted in a complex and multifaceted religious and social environment.

Religion

Hong Kong is characterized by its religious diversity, which is a reflection of its historical, cultural, and demographic factors. The city's major religions include **Buddhism**, **Taoism**, **Confucianism**,

<u>Christianity</u>, and <u>Islam</u>. There is also a considerable number of people who do not identify with any specific religion or consider themselves atheist or agnostic.

Buddhism, Taoism, and Confucianism are often collectively referred to as the "three teachings" and form the core of traditional Chinese religious and philosophical thought. These belief systems have had a profound influence on Hong Kong's cultural practices, rituals, and values. Many Hong Kong residents practice a combination of these faiths, with elements of ancestor worship and folk religion also playing a significant role in their religious life.

Christianity was introduced to Hong Kong during the British colonial era, and it has since become the city's largest minority religion. The Christian community in Hong Kong is diverse, encompassing both Protestant and Catholic denominations, as well as various ethnic and linguistic groups. Christianity has had a notable impact on Hong Kong's education system, with many of the city's prestigious schools founded by Christian missionaries.

Islam is also present in Hong Kong, primarily due to the presence of a sizable community of domestic workers from Southeast Asia, as well as a smaller population of South Asian Muslims who have historical roots in the city.

Values

Hong Kong's values are shaped by its unique blend of Eastern and Western influences, which stem from its history as a British colony and its current status as a Special Administrative Region of China. As a result, the city's values are often characterized by a mix of traditional Chinese virtues and more modern, Western-oriented beliefs.

Key values that are deeply ingrained in Hong Kong society include the importance of family, respect for authority, and the value of education. The Confucian emphasis on filial piety, or loyalty and obedience to one's parents, is a core aspect of the city's familial values. Additionally, the pursuit of educational achievement and social mobility is highly prized, reflecting the belief in the transformative power of education.

At the same time, Hong Kong's exposure to Western values has fostered a more individualistic and entrepreneurial spirit. The city's values also encompass a strong work ethic, adaptability, and a focus on material success and social status.

Social Norms

Hong Kong's social norms are shaped by its diverse cultural influences and the city's status as an international metropolis. Politeness and respect for others are highly valued, with social etiquette often emphasizing the importance of maintaining "face" or preserving one's dignity and reputation in public settings.

The concept of "guanxi," or personal connections and networks, is an important aspect of social life in Hong Kong. Building and maintaining relationships is seen as crucial for personal and professional success, with people often going to great lengths to foster these connections.

Hong Kong is also known for its fast-paced, densely populated urban environment, which has given rise to a unique set of social norms. These include a strong emphasis on personal space and privacy, as well as a general acceptance of the city's hustle and bustle.

Language: Key Phrases and Expressions

These key phrases and expressions provide a glimpse into the unique aspects of Hong Kong's culture, history, and daily life. Familiarizing oneself with these terms can help to better understand and appreciate the city's rich and multifaceted identity.

Key Phrases and Expressions:

- **"One country, two systems"**: A principle formulated by Deng Xiaoping that refers to the governance of Hong Kong and Macau as Special Administrative Regions (SARs) of China. It allows these regions to maintain their own political, legal, and economic systems, separate from mainland China.

- **"Lion Rock Spirit"**: A term that encapsulates Hong Kong's unique spirit of resilience, hard work, and perseverance. It is named after the iconic Lion Rock Mountain in the city.

- **"Dim sum"**: A Cantonese cuisine that consists of small, bite-sized portions of food, usually served in steamer baskets or small plates. Dim sum is a popular dining experience in Hong Kong, often enjoyed with family or friends during a leisurely weekend brunch.

- **"Kowloon"** and **"Hong Kong Island"**: The two main urban areas of Hong Kong, separated by the Victoria Harbour. Kowloon is located on the mainland, while Hong Kong Island is across the harbor to the south.

- **"Cantonese"**: A Chinese language spoken primarily in the Guangdong province of China, as well as in Hong Kong and Macau. It is one of the major languages spoken in Hong Kong.

- **"Feng shui"**: A traditional Chinese practice that seeks to harmonize the human environment with the natural world through the arrangement of space and objects. Feng shui is commonly used in Hong Kong for home and office design, as well as in urban planning.

- **"Guanxi"**: A Chinese term referring to the network of personal connections and relationships that are crucial for personal and professional success in Chinese societies, including Hong Kong.

- **"Tuen Ng Festival"** or **"Dragon Boat Festival"**: An annual traditional Chinese festival celebrated in Hong Kong, featuring dragon boat races, rice dumplings, and various cultural performances.

- **"Lunar New Year"**: The most important Chinese festival, marking the beginning of the lunar calendar. In Hong Kong, it is celebrated with family gatherings, feasts, and various customs to usher in good fortune and prosperity for the new year.
- **"Mid-Autumn Festival"**: A traditional Chinese festival celebrated in Hong Kong, marked by family gatherings, lantern displays, and the sharing of mooncakes.
- "Wet market": A type of fresh food market commonly found in Hong Kong, where shoppers can find a wide variety of fresh produce, meat, seafood, and other daily necessities.
- "MTR": The Mass Transit Railway, Hong Kong's extensive and efficient public transportation system, which includes underground trains, light rail, and buses.

Colloquial expressions:

Here are some common colloquial expressions used in Hong Kong, which often reflect the city's unique linguistic and cultural blend:

- "**Add oil**" (加油, ga yau): A phrase of encouragement similar to "keep it up" or "you can do it" in English. It can be used in various situations, such as cheering someone on or motivating them to continue their efforts.
- **"Chop"** (蓋印, gai yan): Referring to a personal or company seal or stamp. In Hong Kong, it is common to use chops as signatures on official documents or contracts.
- **"Lai see"** (利是, lai si): Red envelopes containing money, traditionally given during Lunar New Year and other special occasions such as weddings or the birth of a child. The money inside is usually given in even amounts to symbolize good luck and prosperity.
- **"Mahjong"** (麻雀, ma jeuk): A traditional Chinese tile-based game, popular in Hong Kong as a social and recreational activity. The game is often played during family gatherings or with friends.
- **"Typhoon Signal No. 8"** (八號風球, baat hou fung kau): A term referring to the Hong Kong Observatory's tropical cyclone warning signal system. When a Typhoon Signal No. 8 is hoisted, most businesses, schools, and public transportation services in the city will be suspended.
- **"Cha chaan teng"** (茶餐廳, cha can teng): A type of casual eatery or café in Hong Kong, serving affordable local dishes such as milk tea, instant noodles, and sandwiches. These establishments are known for their fast service and no-frills atmosphere.
- **"Daai paai dong"** (大牌檔, daai paai dong): Open-air food stalls typically found on streets and in markets, offering a variety of affordable, freshly cooked dishes. These stalls are part of Hong Kong's street food culture.
- **"Wonton noodles"** (雲吞麵, wan tan min): A popular Cantonese dish in Hong Kong, consisting of thin egg noodles served with shrimp or pork-filled wonton dumplings in a clear broth.

- **"Mui jai"** (妹仔, mui zai): A colloquial term for a domestic helper, often referring to women from the Philippines or Indonesia who work in Hong Kong as live-in domestic workers.
- **"Gweilo"** (鬼佬, gwai lou): A Cantonese slang term originally used to refer to foreigners, particularly those of European descent. While it can be considered derogatory, some expatriates in Hong Kong have adopted the term with a sense of humour.)

Famous Residents

Hong Kong has been home to numerous notable historical figures who have contributed to the city's rich history and development. Some of these famous Hong Kong historical residents include:

- **Sir Thomas Jackson:** Sir Thomas Jackson was the third Chief Manager of the Hongkong and Shanghai Banking Corporation (HSBC), serving from 1876 to 1902. Under his leadership, HSBC expanded its presence in Asia and played a significant role in financing the growth of Hong Kong's economy. A statue of Jackson can be found outside the HSBC headquarters in Central, Hong Kong.
- **Sun Yat-sen:** Sun Yat-sen, known as the "Father of Modern China," was a revolutionary leader who played a key role in the overthrow of the Qing Dynasty and the establishment of the Republic of China. Although born in Guangdong province, Sun spent time in Hong Kong for his education and revolutionary activities. He attended the Government Central School (now Queen's College) and later Hong Kong College of Medicine for Chinese (now the University of Hong Kong).
- **Sir Robert Ho Tung:** Sir Robert Ho Tung was a prominent businessman and philanthropist in early 20th century Hong Kong. He was the first person of Chinese descent to be knighted by the British Empire. Ho Tung made significant contributions to Hong Kong's society, particularly in the fields of education, healthcare, and public welfare. The Ho Tung Library at the University of Hong Kong is named in his honour.
- **Bruce Lee:** Bruce Lee, born in San Francisco, spent much of his childhood in Hong Kong before returning to the United States. He is considered one of the most influential martial artists of all time and a significant pop culture icon of the 20th century. His martial arts philosophy and films contributed to the global popularity of Hong Kong cinema and martial arts.
- **Anita Mui:** Anita Mui was a renowned Cantopop singer and actress in Hong Kong, who achieved significant success in the 1980s and 1990s. Known as the "Madonna of the East," Mui was a trailblazer in the Hong Kong entertainment industry, leaving a lasting impact on the city's music and film scene.
- **Sir Run Run Shaw:** Sir Run Run Shaw was a Hong Kong media mogul who co-founded the Shaw Brothers Studio, which played a significant role in shaping the city's film industry. He also established Television Broadcasts Limited (TVB), one of Hong Kong's leading television

broadcasting companies. As a philanthropist, Shaw contributed to numerous educational, medical, and cultural causes in Hong Kong and beyond.

Famous Legends & Myths

Hong Kong, with its rich cultural history and blend of Eastern and Western influences, has its fair share of legends and myths that capture the imagination and reflect the city's unique identity. Some of these famous legends and myths include:

- **Legend of the White Snake**: A popular Chinese legend that has been adapted into various literary works, operas, and films, including some set in Hong Kong. The story revolves around a white snake spirit that transforms into a beautiful woman, who falls in love with a human man. Their love faces numerous challenges, including the disapproval of a powerful Buddhist monk.

- The Dragon and the Pearl: According to this myth, Hong Kong was once inhabited by dragons that protected the people and brought them good fortune. One day, a dragon left behind a shining pearl, which attracted merchants and traders from all around. The pearl is believed to symbolize the prosperity and growth of Hong Kong as an international trade centre.

- The Legend of Lovers' Rock: Lovers' Rock is a famous rock formation located on Bowen Road in Hong Kong Island. The legend associated with this rock tells the story of two star-crossed lovers who, unable to be together due to their differing social status, chose to leap to their deaths from the rock. The rock is now a popular site for locals to pray for good fortune in love and relationships.

- The Repulse Bay Tigers: In the early 20th century, it was rumoured that the area around Repulse Bay was home to a group of man-eating tigers. While there is no solid evidence of tigers ever living in Hong Kong, this urban legend persisted, creating a sense of fear and mystery around the area.

- **Kowloon Walled City**: While not a legend or myth, the Kowloon Walled City was a densely populated, largely ungoverned settlement in Hong Kong, which existed from the 1950s until its demolition in the 1990s. The Walled City has become the subject of numerous urban legends and stories due to its reputation as a haven for crime, poverty, and chaos. It has also inspired various works of fiction, films, and video games.

4. ADAPTING TO DAILY LIFE

Housing and Accommodation

Adapting to daily life in Hong Kong may present challenges for newcomers, particularly in terms of housing and accommodations. The city is known for its high population density and limited land, which has resulted in a competitive housing market and relatively small living spaces.

Types of Housing

There is a variety of housing options in Hong Kong, ranging from high-rise apartments and condominiums to townhouses and village houses. The majority of residents live in high-rise buildings, which can be found throughout the city. Expatriates and more affluent locals may choose to live in gated communities or luxury condominiums, which offer additional facilities such as swimming pools, gyms, and clubhouses.

Location

Choosing the right location for your housing is crucial in Hong Kong, as it can significantly impact your daily life and commute. Popular areas for expatriates include Central, Mid-Levels, and Wan Chai on Hong Kong Island, and Tsim Sha Tsui and Kowloon Tong in Kowloon. These areas offer a mix of residential and commercial properties, with easy access to public transportation, shopping, dining, and entertainment options.

Cost

Hong Kong is known for its high cost of living, with housing being one of the most significant expenses. Rent can vary greatly depending on the location, size, and quality of the property. It is essential to research and compare different neighbourhoods and housing options to find a place that suits your budget and needs.

Public Housing

The Hong Kong government provides public housing for lower-income residents through the Hong Kong Housing Authority. Public housing is typically more affordable than private housing, but there is often a long waiting list for eligible applicants.

Finding a Place

To find suitable housing in Hong Kong, you can consult local real estate agencies, search online property listings, or ask for recommendations from friends or colleagues. It is advisable to view multiple properties before making a decision, as the quality and size of accommodations can vary significantly.

Lease Agreements

Rental contracts in Hong Kong are typically signed for a minimum of one year, with a possible option to renew. Tenants are usually required to pay a security deposit equivalent to two or three months' rent, and sometimes an additional month's rent as an agency fee. It is essential to thoroughly review the lease agreement and negotiate any necessary terms before signing.

Utilities and Bills

In most cases, tenants are responsible for paying their own utility bills, such as electricity, water, and gas. It is important to clarify with the property owner or property agent which expenses are included in the rent, and which are the tenant's responsibility.

Transportation and Getting Around

Hong Kong has an efficient, reliable, and affordable public transportation system, which makes getting around the city relatively easy for expats and locals alike. Here are some key aspects of Hong Kong's transportation system that expats should be familiar with:

Mass Transit Railway (MTR)

The MTR is Hong Kong's extensive subway system, which serves as the backbone of the city's public transportation network. It connects major residential, commercial, and tourist areas across Hong Kong Island, Kowloon, and the New Territories. The MTR is clean, safe, and punctual, making it a popular choice for daily commutes and leisure travel.

Buses

Hong Kong has a comprehensive network of buses, including double-decker buses, minibuses, and single-decker buses, which cover various routes across the city. Bus fares are relatively inexpensive, and many buses are air-conditioned for added comfort. While buses can be slower than the MTR due to traffic, they serve areas not reached by the subway system.

Trams

Operating on Hong Kong Island, the iconic double-decker trams offer a slower-paced, scenic mode of transportation. Trams are an affordable and environmentally-friendly way to explore the city and experience a taste of old Hong Kong.

Taxis

Taxis are plentiful and reasonably priced in Hong Kong. They are color-coded according to their operating areas: red taxis serve urban areas, green taxis serve the New Territories, and blue taxis serve Lantau Island. Expats should note that most taxi drivers speak limited English, so it's helpful to have your destination written in Chinese or use a map to communicate your desired location.

Ferries

Ferries provide a picturesque and leisurely way to travel between Hong Kong Island and Kowloon or to outlying islands such as Lamma, Cheung Chau, and Peng Chau. The most famous ferry route is the Star Ferry, which offers stunning views of the Hong Kong skyline and Victoria Harbour.

Octopus Card

The Octopus Card is a contactless smart card that can be used to pay for fares on most public transportation, including the MTR, buses, trams, and ferries. The card can be easily reloaded at MTR stations, convenience stores, or online, and can also be used for purchases at various shops and restaurants.

Driving

While it is possible to drive in Hong Kong, many expats find it unnecessary due to the city's excellent public transportation system. Traffic can be congested, parking is limited and expensive, and Hong Kong follows the left-hand driving system, which may be unfamiliar to some expats. If you do choose to drive, you'll need a valid Hong Kong driver's license or an International Driving Permit.

Cycling

While cycling is not as popular in Hong Kong as in some other cities, it can be a viable option for short-distance commutes or recreational activities in certain areas. Expats should be aware that Hong Kong's hilly terrain, busy streets, and humid climate can make cycling more challenging.

Education and Schooling Options

Expats living in Hong Kong have access to a variety of education and schooling options for their children, ranging from local public schools to international schools. It is essential to research and compare different schools to find the best fit for your child's needs, learning style, and background. Here are some key aspects of education and schooling options in Hong Kong:

Local Public Schools

Public schools in Hong Kong generally follow the local curriculum, which is taught in Cantonese and emphasizes traditional Chinese values. While these schools are free or low-cost, the language barrier and cultural differences can make it difficult for expat children to integrate and adapt. However, attending a local public school can be an excellent opportunity for children to learn Cantonese and immerse themselves in Hong Kong's culture.

Private Independent Schools

Some private independent schools in Hong Kong offer a more Western-style education, with English as the primary language of instruction. These schools may follow the British,

American, or other international curricula, providing a smoother transition for expat children. However, private independent schools often have higher tuition fees than public schools.

International Schools

International schools are a popular choice for expats in Hong Kong, as they offer globally recognized curricula such as the International Baccalaureate (IB), the British A-Levels, or the American Advanced Placement (AP) program. These schools often have a diverse student body and teaching staff, providing a multicultural learning environment. English is typically the primary language of instruction, though some international schools also offer bilingual programs. While international schools offer high-quality education and facilities, they can be expensive, with tuition fees being significantly higher than local schools.

Preschools and Kindergartens

For younger children, there is a range of preschools and kindergartens available in Hong Kong, including local, private, and international options. These early education institutions typically offer programs for children aged 2 to 6, focusing on foundational learning, socialization, and play.

Special Education Needs (SEN) Support

If your child requires additional support due to learning disabilities or special needs, it is essential to research schools that offer SEN programs or resources. While some international and private schools may have dedicated SEN departments, local public schools may have more limited support available.

School Application and Admission Process

The application and admission process for schools in Hong Kong can be competitive, particularly for international and top private schools. It is crucial to start researching schools and preparing application materials well in advance of your move. Be prepared to provide academic records, letters of recommendation, and other documentation, as well as attend interviews or assessments if required.

Extracurricular Activities

In addition to academics, many schools in Hong Kong offer extracurricular activities to enrich students' learning experiences and foster personal growth. These may include sports, arts, clubs, and community service opportunities.

Healthcare and Medical Facilities

Hong Kong is known for its high-quality healthcare system, with world-class medical facilities and well-trained healthcare professionals. Expats living in the city have access to both public and private healthcare services. Here is an overview of the healthcare system and medical facilities in Hong Kong for expats:

Public Healthcare

Hong Kong has an extensive public healthcare system, operated by the Hospital Authority, which provides heavily subsidized medical care to residents. The public healthcare system includes hospitals, clinics, and other healthcare facilities. To access these services, residents must hold a valid Hong Kong Identity Card. Public healthcare services are generally of high quality, but waiting times can be long for non-emergency treatments and specialist consultations.

Private Healthcare

For expats who prefer faster access to healthcare services or more personalized care, private healthcare is an alternative option. Private hospitals and clinics in Hong Kong offer excellent facilities and shorter waiting times, but at a higher cost compared to public healthcare services. Many expats and locals with private health insurance opt for private healthcare to enjoy more flexibility and choice in their medical care.

Health Insurance

While public healthcare is affordable for residents, many expats choose to have private health insurance to cover the costs of private healthcare services or treatments not covered by the public system. Some employers may provide health insurance as part of an expat's compensation package. If not, it is essential to research and compare different insurance plans and providers to find the most suitable coverage for your needs.

Primary Care

For routine medical care, expats can visit general practitioners (GPs) at private clinics or public outpatient clinics. GPs can treat common illnesses, provide preventive care, and refer patients to specialists if necessary. It is crucial to find a primary care doctor who speaks your preferred language and understands your medical history and needs.

Specialist Care

Hong Kong has a range of specialists available in both the public and private sectors. In the public system, patients generally require a referral from a GP to see a specialist. In the private sector, patients can directly book appointments with specialists, though this can be more expensive.

Emergency Care

In case of a medical emergency, expats can call 999 for an ambulance or go directly to the nearest public hospital's Accident & Emergency (A&E) department. While emergency care is provided at a minimal cost in public hospitals, private hospitals may charge substantial fees for emergency services.

Pharmacies

Pharmacies in Hong Kong are well-stocked with a wide range of over-the-counter and prescription medications. It is essential to have a prescription from a registered medical practitioner to purchase prescription drugs. Some pharmacists may speak English, but it is helpful to have your prescription written in both English and Chinese.

Dental Care

Hong Kong has numerous dental clinics offering high-quality dental care, including general dentistry, orthodontics, and oral surgery. Dental care is generally not covered under the public healthcare system, so patients are expected to pay for these services out-of-pocket or through private dental insurance.

Safety and Security

Hong Kong is generally considered a safe and secure city for expats, with low crime rates and a well-developed infrastructure. However, as with any major urban area, it is essential to be aware of potential safety and security risks and take appropriate precautions. Here are some tips and guidelines for expats to ensure their safety and security in Hong Kong:

General Safety

Hong Kong has a low crime rate, and most areas are safe to explore during the day and night. However, it is essential to remain vigilant, especially in crowded or tourist-heavy areas. Be aware of your surroundings, avoid displaying valuables openly, and keep your belongings secure.

Petty Crime

While violent crime is rare in Hong Kong, petty crimes such as pickpocketing, bag snatching, and scams can occur. To minimize the risk of becoming a target, secure your valuables, avoid carrying large amounts of cash, and be cautious when using ATMs, especially in secluded locations.

Public Transportation Safety

Public transportation in Hong Kong is generally safe and reliable. However, it is essential to be cautious during peak hours when trains and buses can become crowded, making it easier for pickpockets to operate. Always keep your belongings secure and be mindful of your personal space.

Road Safety

Hong Kong follows the left-hand driving system, which may be unfamiliar to some expats. When walking or cycling, always be cautious and follow traffic rules. Pedestrians should look both ways before crossing the street, and cyclists should wear helmets and follow designated bike lanes when available.

Typhoons and Severe Weather

Hong Kong is susceptible to typhoons, particularly during the months of May to November. Be aware of weather warnings and follow the advice of local authorities in the event of a typhoon or severe weather. Make sure you have an emergency plan and supplies in place.

Political Protests

Over the past few years, Hong Kong has experienced a number of large-scale political protests. While these events are typically non-violent, they can lead to disruptions in transportation and public services. Stay informed about any planned demonstrations, avoid protest areas, and follow the advice of local authorities.

Emergency Services

In case of an emergency, dial 999 for police, fire, or ambulance services. It is essential to know the address and contact information of your country's consulate or embassy in Hong Kong for assistance in case of emergencies or other issues.

Personal Security Measures

Take common-sense precautions to protect yourself and your belongings. Install reliable locks on your home and vehicle, do not share personal information with strangers, and be cautious when using social media to share your location or travel plans.

5. NAVIGATING SOCIAL INTERACTIONS AND ETIQUETTE

Making Friends and Building Connections

Navigating social interactions and etiquette is an important aspect of adapting to daily life in another country. Building connections and making friends with locals and other expatriates can greatly enhance your experience and help you acclimate to the culture more quickly. Here are some tips for making friends and building connections while respecting local social etiquette:

Language

Learning some basic phrases can go a long way in making friends and breaking down communication barriers. Even if your language skills are limited, locals will appreciate your effort to speak their language. Additionally, consider enrolling in a language class, which can also serve as an opportunity to meet new people and practice your language skills.

Cultural understanding

Familiarize yourself with local customs, traditions, and social norms to better understand and navigate social interactions. Being aware of and respecting local etiquette, such as greetings, table manners, and gift-giving customs, will help you make a positive impression and build rapport with locals.

Networking events and social clubs

Attend networking events, expatriate meetups, and social clubs to meet like-minded individuals and expand your social circle. There are numerous groups and organizations catering to expatriates, offering opportunities for cultural exchange, language practice, and shared interests.

Hobbies and interests

Pursue your hobbies and interests by joining clubs, teams, or classes. Participating in activities that you enjoy will provide a natural setting to connect with others who share your interests, making it easier to build friendships.

Social media and messaging apps

Social media platforms and messaging apps are usually widely used and can be an excellent tool for staying connected and organizing social events. Be sure to exchange contact information with new acquaintances and join relevant groups to stay informed about upcoming events and activities.

Be open and approachable

When interacting with locals and other expatriates, be open, approachable, and willing to engage in conversation. Share your experiences, ask questions, and show genuine interest in learning about culture and the experiences of others. Demonstrating curiosity and an open-minded attitude will make you more approachable and help you build connections more easily.

Patience and persistence

Building meaningful friendships takes time and effort, especially when navigating cultural differences. Be patient and persistent in your efforts to connect with others and remember that building strong relationships may require additional time and understanding.

Social Customs and Taboos

Hong Kong is a unique blend of Eastern and Western cultures, with deep-rooted Chinese traditions coexisting alongside more modern and cosmopolitan influences. As an expat, it is essential to be aware of local social customs and taboos to navigate social situations with ease and respect. Here are some key social customs and taboos in Hong Kong:

Greetings

A handshake is the standard greeting in Hong Kong, especially in professional settings. However, some locals may nod or bow slightly when greeting others, particularly in more traditional settings. Address people by their titles and surnames, unless invited to use their first names.

Gift-Giving

In Hong Kong, it is common to exchange gifts during social visits or on special occasions such as birthdays or Lunar New Year. When giving or receiving gifts, always use both hands, and do not open gifts immediately in front of the giver. It is considered impolite to give gifts in sets of four, as the number four is associated with bad luck.

Dining Etiquette

When dining with locals, it is essential to be aware of Chinese table manners. Wait for the host to start eating before you begin. Use chopsticks correctly, and do not stick them vertically into your food, as this is associated with funerals. If you are not proficient with chopsticks, it is acceptable to ask for utensils. It is common for dishes to be shared family-style, and it is polite to try a little of each dish. When eating out, the host generally pays the bill, and it is customary for guests to offer to pay or share the cost.

Personal Space

Hong Kong is a densely populated city, and personal space may be limited in public areas. However, it is essential to respect people's personal space and avoid touching others, particularly those of a different sex, unless you have a close relationship.

Public Behaviour

In general, Hong Kong residents value modesty and politeness. Keep your voice down in public places, avoid discussing sensitive topics such as politics or religion, and refrain from displaying excessive affection in public.

Punctuality

Being punctual is essential in Hong Kong, both in professional and social settings. Arriving late to meetings or appointments is considered disrespectful. If you are running late, inform the other party as soon as possible.

Superstitions

Many Hong Kong residents are superstitious and believe in traditional Chinese customs and practices, such as feng shui. Be respectful of these beliefs, even if you do not share them.

Taboos

There are certain taboos to be aware of in Hong Kong. For example, avoid wearing white to social events, as it is associated with mourning. Do not point with your index finger, as this is considered rude. Be cautious when discussing political issues or the relationship between Hong Kong and mainland China, as these topics can be sensitive.

Dining and Food Culture

Hong Kong is renowned for its diverse and vibrant dining and food culture. The city is a melting pot of various culinary influences, including Cantonese, other Chinese regional cuisines, and international flavours. This rich culinary landscape offers something for everyone, from street food to fine dining. Here are some key aspects of Hong Kong's dining and food culture:

Cantonese Cuisine

As the majority of Hong Kong's population is of Cantonese origin, Cantonese cuisine is the most prominent style of cooking in the city. Known for its delicate flavours, Cantonese dishes often feature fresh ingredients, with an emphasis on seafood and vegetables. Some popular Cantonese dishes include **dim sum**, roast meats (such as roast duck and **char siu**), and steamed fish.

Dim Sum

Dim sum is an integral part of Hong Kong's food culture. Traditionally enjoyed during morning or lunchtime, dim sum is a selection of small, bite-sized dishes served in bamboo steamer baskets or on small plates. Popular dim sum items include **har gow** (shrimp dumplings), **siu mai** (pork and shrimp dumplings), and **cha siu bao** (barbecue pork buns).

Street Food

Street food is an essential aspect of Hong Kong's food culture, with numerous food stalls, known as "**dai pai dong**," found across the city. Some popular street food items include **egg waffles**, **curry fish balls**, and **stinky tofu**. Street food is an affordable and delicious way to experience authentic local flavours.

International Cuisine

Hong Kong's cosmopolitan nature means that the city boasts a diverse range of international cuisines. From Japanese sushi to Italian pasta, Indian curries to French pastries, expats can find almost any type of food in Hong Kong.

Tea Culture

Tea plays a significant role in Hong Kong's food culture. Locals enjoy a variety of Chinese teas, such as **oolong**, **green**, and **pu'er**. One of the most popular local beverages is Hong Kong-style milk tea, which is made by brewing strong black tea and mixing it with condensed or evaporated milk.

Cha Chaan Teng

A unique aspect of Hong Kong's food culture is the **cha chaan teng**, a type of casual eatery that serves a mix of Cantonese and Western dishes at affordable prices. These establishments are known for their eclectic menus, which can include items such as instant noodles with luncheon meat, French toast, and baked rice dishes.

Fine Dining

Hong Kong is also known for its thriving fine dining scene, with numerous Michelin-starred restaurants and high-end establishments offering a variety of cuisines. These restaurants often feature innovative dishes and impressive presentations, attracting food enthusiasts from around the world.

Food Festivals and Events

Throughout the year, Hong Kong hosts various food festivals and events, celebrating the city's diverse culinary landscape. These events showcase local and international food and drink

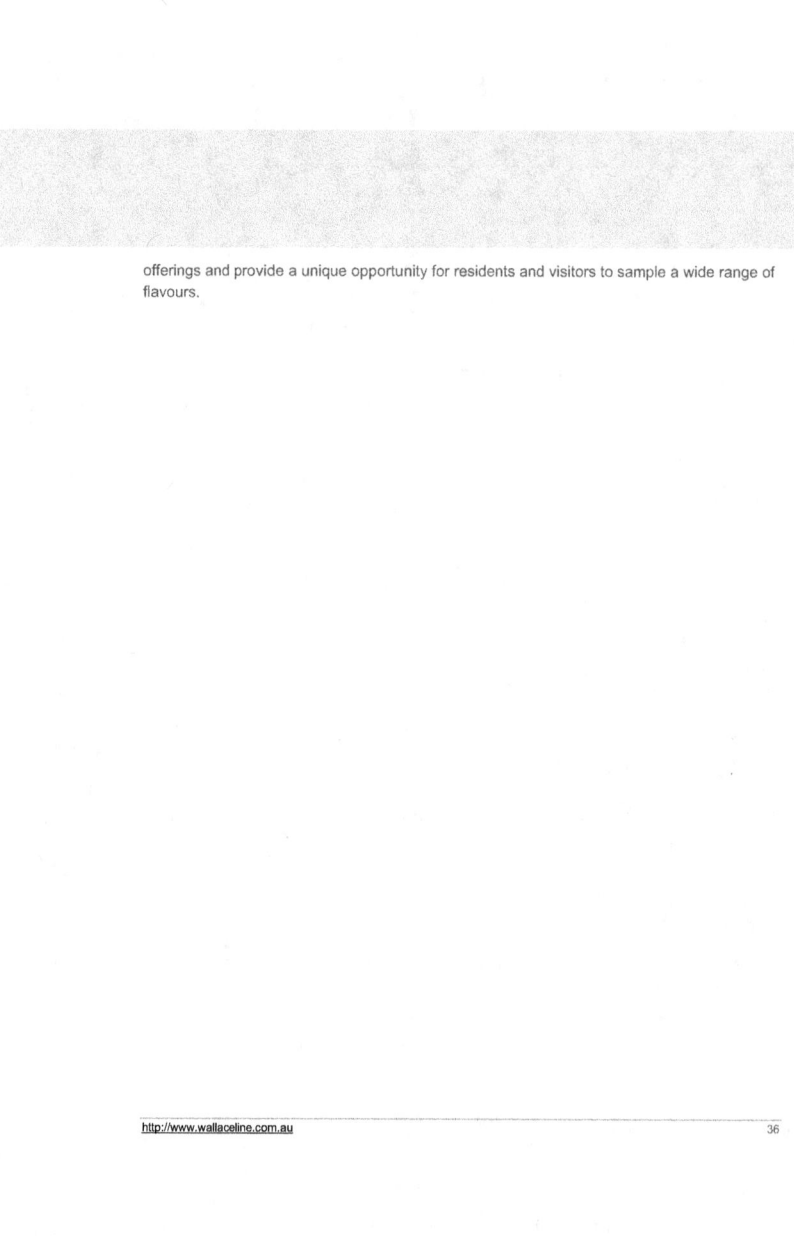

offerings and provide a unique opportunity for residents and visitors to sample a wide range of flavours.

6. BUSINESS ETIQUETTE AND PRACTICES

Building Trust and Relationships

In Hong Kong, as in many other Asian countries, business etiquette and practices are deeply rooted in cultural values and traditions. Building trust and fostering relationships are essential aspects of doing business in the city. Here are some key points to keep in mind when navigating Hong Kong's business environment:

Respect hierarchy

Hong Kong's business culture is generally hierarchical, with great respect accorded to seniority and authority. Be mindful of addressing people by their titles and surnames and show deference to those in higher positions.

Face-to-face meetings

While technology has facilitated remote communication, face-to-face meetings are still highly valued in Hong Kong's business culture. Meeting in person allows for better rapport-building and provides an opportunity to establish trust and credibility.

Building relationships

Cultivating personal relationships, or "guanxi," is crucial in Hong Kong's business culture. Investing time in getting to know your business partners and understanding their background and interests can go a long way in building strong connections. Attend social events and engage in informal conversations to foster personal bonds.

Patience and persistence

Building trust and strong relationships in Hong Kong may take time. Be patient and persistent in your efforts to establish connections and avoid rushing into business discussions or transactions.

Business cards

The exchange of business cards is an essential aspect of Hong Kong's business etiquette. Offer and receive cards using both hands and take a moment to read and acknowledge the information on the card before putting it away. Treat others' cards with respect, as they are seen as an extension of the individual.

Gift-giving

In Hong Kong, gift-giving can be an important part of building relationships and demonstrating goodwill. Consider offering a small, tasteful gift when meeting new business partners or on special occasions. Be aware of cultural sensitivities when selecting gifts and avoid items that may be considered inappropriate, such as clocks or anything in sets of four.

Non-verbal communication

Pay attention to non-verbal cues during meetings and conversations, as they can provide valuable insights into your counterparts' thoughts and feelings. Be aware of your own body language and maintain good eye contact to show interest and engagement.

Saving face

In Hong Kong's business culture, maintaining one's dignity and reputation, or "face," is of utmost importance. Be mindful of your actions and words to avoid causing embarrassment or offense to others. Address any issues or conflicts privately and diplomatically and avoid public confrontations.

Indirect communication

Hong Kong businesspeople may communicate more indirectly than their Western counterparts, using subtle hints or gestures to convey their thoughts. Be attentive to these cues and avoid pressing for direct answers, as doing so may cause discomfort or loss of face.

Dress Code and Appearance

In Hong Kong, appearance and dress code play an important role in conveying professionalism and respect in both business and social settings. As a cosmopolitan city, Hong Kong's dress code is generally a blend of Western and Asian influences. Here are some guidelines on dress code and appearance for various situations:

Business Attire

In most business settings, Hong Kong follows a formal dress code. For men, this typically means wearing a suit, dress shirt, tie, and polished dress shoes. Dark-coloured suits are generally preferred, with lighter colours being more suitable for the warmer months. For women, conservative business suits, dresses, or skirts with blouses are appropriate. Women should avoid overly revealing or tight-fitting clothing.

Casual Attire

In more casual settings, such as weekends or informal social gatherings, Hong Kong residents tend to dress more casually but still maintain a neat and presentable appearance. Men may wear trousers or jeans with collared shirts or polo shirts, while women can opt for dresses, skirts, or trousers with blouses or casual tops. Shorts and flip-flops are generally reserved for the beach or very casual settings.

Social Events

For more formal social events, such as weddings or cocktail parties, men should wear suits or tuxedos, and women should opt for cocktail dresses or evening gowns. It is essential to be aware of any specific dress codes mentioned on event invitations and adhere to them.

Religious and Traditional Settings

When visiting temples, mosques, or other religious or traditional settings, it is important to dress modestly and respectfully. Men should wear trousers and long-sleeved shirts, while women should wear skirts or trousers that cover the knees and tops that cover the shoulders and upper arms.

Personal Grooming

Good personal hygiene and grooming are essential in Hong Kong. Make sure your hair is clean and well-groomed, and avoid excessive use of perfumes or colognes, as strong fragrances may be considered offensive.

Tattoos and Piercings

While tattoos and piercings are becoming more accepted in Hong Kong, particularly among younger generations, they may still be frowned upon in conservative or professional settings. If you have visible tattoos or piercings, consider covering them up or removing them in such situations.

Accessories

In Hong Kong, accessories can be used to express personal style, but they should be kept tasteful and appropriate for the setting. Avoid overly flashy or ostentatious jewellery, particularly in professional environments.

Business Cards

In Hong Kong, business cards play a vital role in establishing professional relationships and making a positive first impression. They are considered an extension of the person and a way to show respect for the individual and their company. Here are some guidelines on the proper use and handling of business cards in Hong Kong:

Design

Business cards should be designed professionally, with clear and easy-to-read fonts. Include your name, title, company name, and contact details. It is also a good idea to have one side of the card printed in English and the other side in Chinese, particularly if you plan to conduct business with Chinese-speaking counterparts.

Quality

Invest in high-quality business cards, as the card's appearance is a reflection of you and your company. Opt for good-quality paper and printing to make a favourable impression.

Exchanging business cards

When exchanging business cards, use both hands to present and receive the card. This gesture is a sign of respect and politeness. If you are sitting, stand up before exchanging cards.

Receiving a business card

Take a moment to read the card and acknowledge the information before putting it away. Making a brief comment or asking a question about the card's content can demonstrate your interest and attentiveness.

Storing business cards

Always store business cards in a cardholder or a designated section of your wallet or purse. Avoid folding, writing on, or otherwise damaging the cards, as this can be seen as disrespectful.

Timing

The best time to exchange business cards is at the beginning of a meeting or after introductions. If you are attending a business event or a networking session, have a sufficient number of cards on hand to exchange with new contacts.

Cultural sensitivity

Be aware of cultural differences when exchanging business cards with people from other countries or backgrounds. Some individuals may have specific customs or preferences regarding the exchange of business cards, and respecting these can help establish rapport and trust.

Introductions

In Hong Kong, business introductions are an essential aspect of building professional relationships and establishing trust with new contacts. Understanding and adhering to the local etiquette when making introductions can help ensure a smooth start to your business interactions. Here are some guidelines to follow when making business introductions in Hong Kong:

Hierarchy and seniority

In Hong Kong's business culture, hierarchy and seniority are highly respected. When making introductions, always introduce the person with the highest rank or position first, followed by those with lower ranks. This applies to both individuals from your company and those from the company you are meeting.

Use titles and surnames

When introducing someone, address them using their title (such as Mr., Mrs., Dr., or Director) and their surname. If you are unsure of their title, it is safer to use "Mr." or "Ms." followed by their surname. Using a person's first name during the initial introduction may be considered too informal or disrespectful, especially in more formal business settings.

Shake hands

A firm handshake is a standard greeting during business introductions in Hong Kong. Remember to shake hands with each person present, starting with the highest-ranking individual. Maintain good eye contact and offer a warm smile during the handshake.

Exchange business cards

After making an introduction and shaking hands, it is customary to exchange business cards. Follow the guidelines for exchanging business cards, as mentioned in the previous answer, to ensure proper etiquette.

Be attentive

During introductions, pay attention to the names and titles of the individuals you are meeting. This will not only demonstrate your interest but will also help you remember their names for future interactions.

Small talk

Engaging in small talk is an essential aspect of building rapport in Hong Kong's business culture. After introductions, you may engage in light conversation about topics such as the weather, local news, or any recent events. Avoid controversial topics or overly personal questions.

Show respect

Demonstrate respect for your counterparts by maintaining a polite and attentive demeanour throughout the meeting. Be punctual, as arriving late can be seen as disrespectful.

Language considerations

While English is widely spoken in Hong Kong's business circles, it is helpful to learn some basic Cantonese phrases to show respect and interest in your counterparts' culture. A simple greeting or thank you in Cantonese can go a long way in making a positive impression.

Communication Styles and Nonverbal Cues

In Hong Kong, communication styles can be influenced by a combination of traditional Chinese values, such as Confucianism, and the city's British colonial history. Understanding the nuances of Hong Kong's communication styles and being aware of nonverbal cues can help expats navigate the local culture more effectively. Here are some key aspects to consider:

Indirect communication

Hong Kong's communication style tends to be more indirect and subtle compared to Western cultures. People often use nonverbal cues, context, and indirect expressions to convey their message, as it helps maintain harmony and avoid conflicts. Expats should pay close attention to these cues and be patient when trying to understand their counterparts' intentions.

Politeness and face-saving

Saving face is an essential concept in Hong Kong's culture. People often avoid confrontation and direct criticism to preserve their own and others' dignity. Expats should also be mindful of this concept and avoid causing embarrassment or making others feel uncomfortable.

Hierarchy and respect

Hierarchy and respect for authority play a significant role in Hong Kong's communication style. People may be more reserved when speaking to someone with a higher status, and deference is expected in such interactions. Be aware of this dynamic and act accordingly to maintain good relations.

Nonverbal cues

Nonverbal communication is crucial in Hong Kong. Expats should be aware of their facial expressions, gestures, and body language, as these can convey messages just as effectively as words. Some common nonverbal cues in Hong Kong include:

- Avoiding direct eye contact, which may be seen as a sign of disrespect or aggression
- Nodding or bowing slightly when greeting someone as a sign of respect
- Maintaining a respectful distance during conversations to show personal boundaries

Silence and listening

In Hong Kong, silence is not necessarily a negative thing. It can be an indication that the person is listening carefully or contemplating their response. Expats should learn to be comfortable with silence and not feel the need to fill every gap in the conversation.

Tone of voice

The tone of voice is also essential in Hong Kong's communication. Speaking in a calm, respectful, and measured manner can help build trust and rapport. Avoid raising your voice or sounding aggressive, as this can be seen as disrespectful.

Gestures and physical touch

Physical touch is generally limited in professional settings in Hong Kong. Avoid overly familiar gestures such as hugging or patting someone on the back, as this can be seen as intrusive or inappropriate.

7. OFFICE CULTURE AND HIERARCHIES

Respect for Authority and Seniority

In Hong Kong's office culture, respect for authority and seniority is deeply ingrained and plays a significant role in daily interactions. The influence of Confucianism, which emphasizes harmony, hierarchy, and respect for elders, can be seen in the way people conduct themselves in the workplace. Here are some aspects to consider when navigating office culture and hierarchies in Hong Kong:

Hierarchical structures

Organizations in Hong Kong tend to have well-defined hierarchical structures, with clear roles and responsibilities for each employee. Decisions are usually made by those in higher positions, and subordinates are expected to respect and follow their directives.

Respectful communication

When addressing or speaking to someone in a higher position or with more seniority, it is important to show respect and deference. Use formal titles and surnames when addressing superiors and avoid interrupting or openly disagreeing with them in public. Instead, voice your concerns or suggestions privately and diplomatically.

Decision-making process:

The decision-making process in Hong Kong's office culture is often top-down, with senior management making most of the decisions. Employees at lower levels are generally expected to execute tasks rather than question or challenge the decisions of their superiors.

Face-saving

Saving face is a crucial aspect of office culture in Hong Kong. Avoid publicly criticizing or challenging someone in a higher position, as this can cause them to lose face and damage your professional relationship. Instead, find a private and respectful way to address any concerns or issues.

Protocol and etiquette

Following proper protocol and etiquette when interacting with superiors is essential in Hong Kong's office culture. This may include waiting for your superior to initiate a handshake, offering them a seat before taking one yourself, or allowing them to enter or exit a room first.

Mentorship and guidance

In many Hong Kong workplaces, senior employees are expected to provide mentorship and guidance to their juniors. This relationship is built on mutual respect, with the junior employee learning from their senior's experience and wisdom, while the senior employee is expected to support and nurture the junior's growth and development.

Delegation and responsibility

In a hierarchical office culture, tasks and responsibilities are often delegated to lower-level employees. It is essential for expats to understand their role in the organization and carry out their tasks diligently, while also respecting the chain of command.

Decision-Making Processes

Decision-making processes in Hong Kong's business environment are typically influenced by the local culture, which emphasizes hierarchy, respect for authority, and the concept of face-saving. Here are some key aspects of the decision-making processes in Hong Kong:

Top-down approach

Decisions are often made at the highest levels of management and then communicated down the chain of command. Lower-level employees are generally expected to follow instructions and execute tasks, rather than question or challenge the decisions of their superiors.

Group consensus

Although the top-down approach is prevalent, group consensus is also valued in Hong Kong's business culture. Superiors may consult with their team members to gather input and opinions before making a final decision. However, the ultimate decision-making power still resides with the higher authorities.

Indirect communication

In the decision-making process, Hong Kong professionals may communicate their opinions and concerns indirectly to avoid confrontation and maintain harmony. Expats should pay attention to nonverbal cues, read between the lines, and be patient in understanding the underlying message.

Relationship-building

Building strong relationships with your Hong Kong counterparts can significantly influence the decision-making process. Establishing trust and rapport through frequent communication and face-to-face meetings can help facilitate smoother decision-making and problem-solving.

Time and patience

Decision-making in Hong Kong may take longer than in Western business cultures due to the emphasis on group consensus, indirect communication, and relationship-building. Expats should be prepared to invest time and patience in navigating the decision-making process.

Formality and protocol

Adhering to proper protocol and formalities is important during the decision-making process. Showing respect to superiors and maintaining appropriate etiquette can help ensure a positive outcome.

Saving face

The concept of face-saving plays a crucial role in Hong Kong's decision-making processes. Professionals avoid public criticism or confrontation to preserve their own and others' dignity. When discussing issues or disagreements, approach the matter privately and diplomatically to maintain harmonious working relationships.

8. BUSINESS MEETINGS AND NEGOTIATIONS

Scheduling and Punctuality

In Hong Kong's business environment, scheduling and punctuality are highly valued and can significantly impact the success of business meetings and negotiations. Here are some key aspects to consider when scheduling and attending meetings in Hong Kong:

Advance scheduling

Business meetings should be scheduled well in advance, preferably two to three weeks prior to the desired date. This allows all parties to plan their schedules accordingly and ensures the availability of key decision-makers.

Written confirmation

Once a meeting date and time have been agreed upon, it is a good idea to send a written confirmation to all participants, outlining the meeting's purpose, agenda, and any relevant materials. This not only serves as a reminder but also helps attendees prepare for the meeting.

Punctuality

Being punctual is essential in Hong Kong's business culture, as it demonstrates respect and professionalism. Arriving late to a meeting may be perceived as a sign of disrespect and could negatively impact the business relationship. Make sure to plan your travel time accordingly and notify your counterparts if you anticipate any delays.

Time management

Hong Kong professionals value efficiency and effective time management during meetings. It is crucial to stick to the agreed-upon schedule and avoid deviating from the agenda. Meetings typically start and end on time, so ensure you cover all essential topics within the allotted timeframe.

Flexibility

Although punctuality and scheduling are vital, expats should also be prepared to adapt to any unexpected changes or rescheduling. Flexibility and a positive attitude can help maintain a harmonious business relationship despite any unforeseen circumstances.

Time of day

Avoid scheduling meetings during lunchtime (usually between 1:00 PM and 2:00 PM) or too late in the afternoon, as it may be difficult for participants to focus. Morning meetings are generally preferred, as attendees are more alert and engaged.

Holidays and weekends

Be mindful of public holidays and weekends when scheduling meetings in Hong Kong. Avoid scheduling meetings during major holidays such as Lunar New Year or Mid-Autumn Festival, as many businesses may be closed or operating with limited staff.

Meeting Structure and Protocol

Understanding the meeting structure and protocol is essential for successful business interactions in Hong Kong. Here are some key aspects of meeting structure and protocol in Hong Kong's business environment:

Greetings and introductions

Begin meetings with a handshake and a slight bow, while maintaining eye contact. Address your counterparts using their formal titles and surnames, unless invited to do otherwise. During introductions, it is customary to exchange business cards, which should be presented and received with both hands.

Seating arrangements

Seating arrangements in meetings are typically based on seniority and hierarchy. The most senior person usually sits at the head of the table, with others arranged according to their rank. Wait for your host to indicate where you should sit, and do not change your seat without permission.

Starting the meeting

The meeting is usually initiated by the most senior person present, who may give a brief opening speech or introduction. Allow your Hong Kong counterparts to set the pace and tone of the meeting.

Agenda

Meetings in Hong Kong generally follow a pre-set agenda. Stick to the agenda and avoid introducing unrelated topics, as this can be seen as inefficient and disrespectful. Make sure all relevant materials and documents are prepared in advance and distributed to attendees, as necessary.

Decision-making

Decisions are often made by the highest-ranking person or collectively after reaching a consensus. Be prepared for a slower decision-making process than in Western cultures, as Hong Kong businesspeople prioritize relationship-building, group consensus, and face-saving.

Respectful communication

Show respect and deference when addressing or speaking to someone with more seniority. Avoid interrupting or openly disagreeing with others, especially those in higher positions. Instead, voice your concerns or suggestions privately and diplomatically.

Nonverbal cues

Pay attention to nonverbal cues during meetings, as Hong Kong businesspeople may communicate indirectly to maintain harmony and save face. Listen carefully, observe body language, and be patient in understanding the underlying message.

Closing the meeting

At the end of the meeting, the most senior person present will typically summarize the key points and decisions made. Express your gratitude for the opportunity to meet and discuss the matters at hand.

Tips for Effective Negotiation

Negotiating effectively in Hong Kong's business environment requires an understanding of the local culture and customs. Here are some tips for effective negotiation in Hong Kong:

Relationship-building

Building strong relationships with your Hong Kong counterparts is crucial for successful negotiations. Invest time in getting to know your business partners through face-to-face meetings, social events, and regular communication. Trust and rapport can significantly influence the negotiation process.

Patience and persistence

Negotiations in Hong Kong may take longer than in Western cultures due to the emphasis on relationship-building, group consensus, and face-saving. Be patient and persistent in pursuing your goals, while also respecting the local customs and practices.

Indirect communication

Hong Kong businesspeople may communicate their opinions and concerns indirectly to maintain harmony and save face. Pay attention to nonverbal cues and read between the lines to understand their underlying message. Be prepared to ask open-ended questions and listen carefully to their responses.

Respect for hierarchy

Show respect and deference to those with more seniority during negotiations. Address them using their formal titles and surnames and avoid openly challenging their views. Instead, express your concerns or suggestions diplomatically and privately.

Compromise and flexibility

Be willing to compromise and show flexibility during negotiations. Demonstrating a willingness to find a mutually beneficial solution can help build trust and strengthen your business relationship.

Face-saving

Be mindful of the concept of face-saving in Hong Kong's business culture. Avoid publicly criticizing or embarrassing your counterparts, as this can damage the relationship and negatively impact negotiations. Instead, address any disagreements or concerns privately and tactfully.

Preparation

Be well-prepared for negotiations by conducting thorough research on your counterparts, their business practices, and the local market conditions. This will help you make informed decisions and present a strong case during negotiations.

Use of intermediaries

In some cases, using intermediaries or third-party negotiators can help facilitate the negotiation process, particularly if there are language barriers or cultural differences. These intermediaries can help bridge communication gaps and ensure that both parties understand each other's needs and expectations.

Common Mistakes to Avoid

When conducting business in Hong Kong, expats should be aware of potential pitfalls and avoid making common mistakes that could negatively impact their professional relationships or business dealings. Here are some common mistakes to avoid:

Disrespecting hierarchy

Hong Kong's business culture places significant importance on hierarchy and seniority. Failing to show respect and deference to those in higher positions can damage your professional relationships. Always address superiors by their titles and surnames and avoid openly challenging their opinions.

Ignoring the concept of face-saving

Disregarding the importance of face-saving can lead to misunderstandings and strain business relationships. Avoid public criticism or confrontation and address any disagreements privately and diplomatically.

Being too direct

Hong Kong professionals often communicate indirectly to maintain harmony and save face. Being overly direct or confrontational may cause discomfort or offense. Adapt your communication style to be subtler and indirect when necessary.

Arriving late to meetings

Punctuality is highly valued in Hong Kong's business culture. Being late to a meeting can be perceived as disrespectful and unprofessional. Always arrive on time or early and notify your counterparts if you anticipate any delays.

Overlooking nonverbal cues

In a culture where indirect communication is common, nonverbal cues play a crucial role. Failing to pay attention to body language, facial expressions, or tone of voice can lead to misunderstandings. Be observant and sensitive to these cues to better understand your counterparts' thoughts and feelings.

Neglecting relationship-building

Hong Kong's business environment emphasizes the importance of personal relationships. Focusing solely on business transactions without investing time in building trust and rapport can hinder your professional success. Attend social events, engage in small talk, and maintain regular communication to strengthen your business relationships.

Failing to prepare

Thorough preparation is essential for successful negotiations and meetings. Neglecting to research your counterparts, their business practices, and local market conditions can put you at a disadvantage. Be well-prepared to present a strong case and make informed decisions.

Underestimating the importance of etiquette

Proper business etiquette and protocol are vital in Hong Kong. Ignoring these customs, such as the appropriate exchange of business cards or adhering to proper dress code, can reflect poorly on your professionalism and negatively impact your business dealings.

9. BUSINESS DINING AND ENTERTAINMENT

Traditional Hospitality

Hong Kong's traditional hospitality reflects a mix of Chinese customs and British colonial influences. The local culture emphasizes politeness, respect, and generosity when hosting guests or interacting with others. Here are some key aspects of traditional hospitality in Hong Kong:

Respect

Hong Kong people value respect and often show it through gestures, such as a slight bow when greeting someone or offering a gift with both hands. They also demonstrate respect by addressing individuals with their formal titles and surnames, unless invited to do otherwise.

Tea

Tea plays a significant role in Hong Kong's hospitality. Serving tea to guests is a common gesture of welcome in both homes and business settings. When visiting someone's home or attending a business meeting, it is customary to be offered tea, which should be accepted politely. If you are the guest of honour, wait for your host to take the first sip before you begin drinking.

Gifts

Offering gifts is an important aspect of Hong Kong's traditional hospitality. When visiting someone's home, it is customary to bring a small gift, such as fruit, pastries, or chocolates, to show appreciation for the host's hospitality. Similarly, in a business setting, exchanging gifts can be a way of building rapport and fostering professional relationships.

Food

Hong Kong people take pride in their diverse and delicious cuisine. When hosting guests, it is common to offer a generous amount of food, often more than can be consumed. As a guest, it is polite to try a little of everything and compliment the host on the meal. However, do not finish everything on your plate, as this may be interpreted as a sign that you are still hungry, and the host has not provided enough food.

Invitations

When extending an invitation to an event or gathering, Hong Kong people usually provide ample notice and expect an RSVP to confirm attendance. If you are invited to someone's home or an event, respond promptly and graciously, even if you are unable to attend.

Courtesy and modesty

Hong Kong's traditional hospitality values courtesy and modesty. When receiving compliments, it is customary to downplay one's achievements or abilities to demonstrate humility. Likewise, avoid boasting or making exaggerated claims, as this may be perceived as arrogance.

Personal space

Hong Kong's dense population has influenced the way people perceive personal space. While locals are generally accustomed to close quarters, be mindful of maintaining a respectful distance when interacting with others, especially in more formal settings.

10. LEISURE, ENTERTAINMENT AND FAMILY ACTIVITIES

Exploring Natural Wonders

Hong Kong is not only a bustling metropolis but also home to a surprising number of natural wonders. With over 40% of its territory consisting of protected country parks, Hong Kong offers a wealth of outdoor activities and picturesque landscapes to explore. Here are some must-visit natural wonders in Hong Kong:

Victoria Peak

Offering a panoramic view of Hong Kong's skyline, Victoria Peak is the highest point on Hong Kong Island. You can take the Peak Tram, which has been operating since 1888, to reach the summit and enjoy breathtaking views of the city and harbor below.

Sai Kung East Country Park

This park, located in the New Territories, is known for its pristine beaches, volcanic rock formations, and hiking trails. The park boasts crystal-clear waters and abundant marine life, making it an excellent spot for snorkelling and diving.

Hong Kong UNESCO Global Geopark

Spread across eight locations, this geopark showcases Hong Kong's unique geological heritage. Highlights include hexagonal rock columns at the High Island Reservoir, the "Devil's Fist" at Port Island, and the "Pineapple Bun Rock" at Tung Ping Chau Island.

Lantau Island

The largest of Hong Kong's islands, Lantau offers a range of natural attractions. Visit Tai O, a traditional fishing village, explore the lush forests and waterfalls of Lantau South Country Park, or hike up to the Tian Tan Buddha, a massive bronze statue overlooking the island.

Tai Long Wan

Often regarded as Hong Kong's most beautiful beach, Tai Long Wan is a secluded bay located in Sai Kung Peninsula. The beach is only accessible by foot or boat, offering a pristine and tranquil escape from the city's hustle and bustle.

Mai Po Nature Reserve

A haven for migratory birds, Mai Po Nature Reserve is situated along the north-western coast of the New Territories. The reserve features extensive mangroves, mudflats, and floating boardwalks, offering a unique opportunity to observe diverse bird species and other wildlife.

Dragon's Back Trail

Named for its undulating ridgeline, Dragon's Back Trail is a popular hiking route offering stunning coastal views. The trail, part of the larger Hong Kong Trail, traverses Shek O Country Park and ends at the picturesque Big Wave Bay.

Plover Cove Reservoir Country Park

Located in the north-eastern part of the New Territories, this park is home to the Plover Cove Reservoir, Hong Kong's second-largest reservoir. The park offers a variety of trails, including the popular Plover Cove Reservoir Family Walk and the more challenging Pat Sin Leng Nature Trail.

Historic Sites and Cultural Attractions

Hong Kong is a city steeped in history and culture, with numerous historic sites and cultural attractions that showcase its rich past and diverse influences. Here are some of the top historic sites and cultural attractions to explore in Hong Kong:

The Peak

This iconic Hong Kong landmark offers stunning views of the city's skyline and harbor. A ride on the historic Peak Tram is a must-do activity, and The Peak Tower features a variety of shops, dining options, and entertainment.

Tsim Sha Tsui Promenade

The promenade offers a breathtaking view of Hong Kong's skyline and Victoria Harbour. The Avenue of Stars, Hong Kong's version of Hollywood's Walk of Fame, features handprints and statues of famous Hong Kong film stars.

Man Mo Temple

Built in the 19th century, this temple is dedicated to the Taoist gods of literature (Man) and war (Mo). The temple's atmospheric interior, filled with incense coils and traditional Chinese architecture, is a peaceful oasis amid the bustling city.

Hong Kong Museum of History

This comprehensive museum chronicles Hong Kong's history, from its geological origins to the present day. The museum's exhibits include artifacts, multimedia displays, and dioramas that bring the past to life.

Tai O Fishing Village

This picturesque village on Lantau Island offers a glimpse into Hong Kong's traditional fishing culture. Visitors can explore the village's stilt houses, sample local seafood delicacies, and take a boat tour to spot the elusive pink dolphins.

Wong Tai Sin Temple

This popular temple is dedicated to Wong Tai Sin, a Taoist deity believed to grant wishes. The temple's ornate architecture and lush gardens make it a popular destination for both tourists and locals seeking good fortune.

Chi Lin Nunnery and Nan Lian Garden

This tranquil Buddhist complex, set amid the bustling city, features stunning Tang Dynasty-style architecture, meticulously landscaped gardens, and peaceful lotus ponds. The nunnery and garden offer a serene respite from the urban surroundings.

Ten Thousand Buddhas Monastery

Located in Sha Tin, this unique site features over 10,000 Buddha statues in various sizes and poses. The steep climb to the monastery offers sweeping views of the surrounding area, and the monastery itself is a remarkable testament to Buddhist devotion.

Hong Kong Heritage Museum

This museum showcases the art, history, and culture of Hong Kong and the surrounding region. Exhibits include traditional Chinese art, Cantonese opera, and the fascinating Bruce Lee: Kung Fu, Art, Life exhibition.

Central and Western Heritage Trail

This walking trail takes visitors through Hong Kong's historic Central and Western districts, exploring a mix of colonial architecture, traditional Chinese temples, and modern skyscrapers.

Family-Friendly Activities and Entertainment

Hong Kong offers a wide range of family-friendly activities and entertainment options, catering to visitors of all ages. Here are some top family-friendly attractions to enjoy in Hong Kong:

Hong Kong Disneyland

This world-famous theme park is a must-visit for families. With its iconic attractions, shows, and beloved Disney characters, Hong Kong Disneyland provides a magical experience for children and adults alike.

Ocean Park

This popular amusement park combines thrilling rides, marine life exhibits, and animal encounters. Ocean Park is home to various species, including giant pandas, dolphins, and seals, providing an educational and entertaining experience for the whole family.

Ngong Ping 360

This cable car ride offers stunning panoramic views of Lantau Island, including the Tian Tan Buddha and Po Lin Monastery. The Ngong Ping Village at the top features shops, dining options, and family-friendly attractions like the multimedia Walking with Buddha exhibit.

Kowloon Park

This large park in Tsim Sha Tsui offers a variety of family-friendly amenities, including playgrounds, an aviary, a swimming pool, and lush gardens. The park also hosts cultural events and performances throughout the year.

Hong Kong Science Museum

This interactive museum features over 500 exhibits, many of which are hands-on and designed for children. The museum covers various scientific topics, from robotics to transportation, making learning fun and engaging for the whole family.

Hong Kong Space Museum

This unique museum offers a fascinating exploration of space and astronomy. The museum features exhibits on space technology, a planetarium, and a variety of educational programs for children.

Snoopy's World

Located in the New Town Plaza shopping mall in Sha Tin, Snoopy's World is a small, Peanuts-themed amusement park featuring statues of beloved characters, themed play areas, and a canoe ride.

Stanley Market and Ma Hang Park

The picturesque seaside town of Stanley is home to a bustling market, where families can shop for souvenirs and local crafts. Nearby Ma Hang Park offers playgrounds, scenic coastal trails, and bird-watching opportunities.

Hong Kong Wetland Park

This eco-tourism park in the New Territories features a variety of habitats, including mangroves, mudflats, and ponds. The park offers educational exhibits, themed walking trails, and bird-watching opportunities for families interested in learning about local ecology.

Hong Kong Zoological and Botanical Gardens

This historic garden in Central Hong Kong is home to a variety of animals, including primates, birds, and reptiles. The garden also features a beautiful collection of plants and flowers, providing a tranquil oasis in the heart of the city.

Celebrations and Festivals

Hong Kong boasts a vibrant cultural scene, with numerous celebrations and festivals taking place throughout the year. These events highlight the city's rich heritage and showcase the diverse influences that have shaped its unique identity. Here are some of the most popular celebrations and festivals in Hong Kong:

Chinese New Year (January/February)

This is the most important festival in the Chinese calendar, celebrated with lion and dragon dances, colourful parades, and spectacular fireworks. Families come together for festive meals and exchange red envelopes containing money for good luck.

Spring Lantern Festival (February)

Marking the end of the Chinese New Year celebrations, the Lantern Festival is celebrated by displaying colourful lanterns, solving riddles, and enjoying traditional foods like glutinous rice balls (tangyuan).

Hong Kong Arts Month (March)

This month-long celebration showcases the city's thriving arts scene, featuring events such as Art Basel Hong Kong, Asia Contemporary Art Show, and Hong Kong International Film Festival.

Ching Ming Festival (April)

Also known as Tomb-Sweeping Day, this festival involves families visiting the graves of their ancestors to clean the tombs, pay respects, and make offerings of food and incense.

Cheung Chau Bun Festival (April/May)

Held on the island of Cheung Chau, this unique festival features parades, lion dances, and the famous Bun Scrambling Competition, where participants climb giant bamboo towers covered in steamed buns.

Dragon Boat Festival (June)

This exciting event is celebrated with colourful dragon boat races across Hong Kong's waterways. Teams compete in traditional long boats, cheered on by crowds of spectators. The festival also includes traditional food like rice dumplings (zongzi) and various cultural performances.

Hungry Ghost Festival (August/September)

During this festival, it is believed that the spirits of the deceased return to the mortal world. Offerings of food, incense, and paper money are made to appease the wandering ghosts, while traditional Chinese operas and music performances are held to entertain them.

Mid-Autumn Festival (September/October)

This harvest festival is celebrated with mooncakes, lantern displays, and family gatherings. The iconic symbol of the festival is the full moon, representing unity and togetherness.

Hong Kong Wine & Dine Festival (October/November)

This annual event showcases the city's culinary expertise, with wine tastings, food pairings, and live entertainment. The festival attracts local and international chefs, offering a wide variety of cuisine and beverages.

WinterFest (December)

Hong Kong embraces the festive spirit with dazzling light displays, Christmas markets, and seasonal events during WinterFest. The city's skyline is illuminated with festive decorations, making it a magical time to visit.

11. PRACTICAL TIPS FOR TRAVELLERS AND EXPATS

Safety and Security Tips

Hong Kong is generally considered a safe city for expats, with low crime rates and a well-organized infrastructure. However, it's essential to take precautions and stay informed to ensure your safety and security while living in the city. Here are some safety and security tips for expats in Hong Kong:

Be aware of your surroundings

Pay attention to your surroundings, especially in crowded areas or when using public transportation. Keep an eye on your belongings and avoid displaying expensive items or large amounts of cash.

Use registered transportation services

Use registered taxis or reputable ride-hailing apps and avoid accepting rides from strangers. When taking public transportation, familiarize yourself with routes and schedules to avoid getting lost.

Be cautious when using ATMs

Use ATMs located in well-lit, busy areas, and be aware of your surroundings when withdrawing cash. Always shield your PIN and be cautious of anyone offering assistance.

Avoid walking alone at night

Although Hong Kong is generally safe, it's best to avoid walking alone in unfamiliar or poorly lit areas at night. Stick to well-travelled streets, and if you feel unsafe, take a taxi or use public transportation.

Be mindful of local customs and laws

Familiarize yourself with local customs, social norms, and laws to avoid inadvertently offending others or getting into trouble. Be respectful of local culture and traditions, particularly when visiting religious sites.

Stay informed about local news and events

Keep up to date with local news, weather forecasts, and public announcements. This will help you stay informed about any potential safety or security concerns, such as political demonstrations, natural disasters, or public health emergencies.

Keep emergency contact information handy

Save the contact information for your country's embassy or consulate, local emergency services, and a reliable local friend or colleague. This will be useful in case of emergencies or if you require assistance.

Register with your embassy

Register with your country's embassy or consulate in Hong Kong to receive updates on safety and security information, as well as assistance in case of emergencies.

Purchase travel or health insurance

Ensure that you have appropriate insurance coverage for your stay in Hong Kong, including health and travel insurance. This will provide financial protection in case of accidents, illness, or other unforeseen circumstances.

Practice good digital security

Protect your personal information online by using strong, unique passwords for your accounts, enabling two-factor authentication, and being cautious when using public Wi-Fi networks.

Healthcare and insurance

As Healthcare in Hong Kong is known for its high standards and modern facilities. The city has a dual healthcare system, consisting of both public and private sectors. Expats living in Hong Kong may have access to both systems, but it's essential to understand how they work and to consider obtaining appropriate health insurance.

Public Healthcare:

The public healthcare system in Hong Kong is operated by the Hospital Authority, which oversees the city's public hospitals and clinics. The public system offers affordable healthcare services to residents, including expats with a valid Hong Kong Identity Card. However, public hospitals prioritize Hong Kong residents, and waiting times can be long, especially for non-urgent cases.

Private Healthcare:

Private healthcare in Hong Kong is known for its excellent quality and personalized care. Private hospitals and clinics offer shorter waiting times, more privacy, and a wider range of specialist services. However, private healthcare can be costly, so it's important to consider health insurance if you plan to use private facilities.

Health Insurance:

Many employers in Hong Kong provide health insurance coverage as part of their benefits package. If your employer does not offer health insurance, or if you want additional coverage, you should consider purchasing a private health insurance plan. There are many local and international insurance companies operating in Hong Kong, offering various coverage levels and options to suit your needs.

When selecting health insurance, consider the following factors:

- Coverage: Ensure that your insurance plan covers a wide range of medical services, including hospitalization, outpatient care, specialist consultations, and emergency medical evacuation if necessary.
- Network: Choose an insurance provider with a broad network of healthcare providers in Hong Kong, including both public and private hospitals and clinics. This will give you more flexibility and choice in selecting healthcare providers.
- Pre-existing conditions: If you have pre-existing medical conditions, check whether your insurance plan covers them or if there is a waiting period before coverage begins.
- Family coverage: If you have dependents, consider a family plan that covers your spouse and children. Some insurance providers offer discounts or additional benefits for family coverage.
- Portability: If you are an expat who travels frequently or plans to move to another country, look for an insurance plan that offers international coverage or can be transferred to another country.
- Cost: Compare the premiums, deductibles, co-payments, and coverage limits of different insurance plans to find one that suits your budget and needs.

12. OVERCOMING STEREOTYPES AND PREJUDICES

Common Misconceptions and Stereotypes

There are several common misconceptions and stereotypes about Hong Kong that may not accurately represent the city or its people. Here are some of the most common myths and stereotypes:

Hong Kong is just a concrete jungle

While Hong Kong is known for its iconic skyline and densely populated urban areas, the city also boasts extensive green spaces, nature reserves, and picturesque hiking trails. In fact, about 40% of Hong Kong's land area is protected as country parks and nature reserves.

Hong Kong is only about business and finance

Although Hong Kong is an important global financial centre, the city offers much more than business opportunities. It has a rich cultural heritage, a thriving arts scene, diverse culinary offerings, and various leisure activities for residents and visitors alike.

Everyone speaks English

Although English is one of the official languages of Hong Kong and many people can speak English, especially in the business world, it's important to remember that Cantonese is the most widely spoken language in the city. Learning some basic Cantonese phrases can help you navigate daily life and show respect for local culture.

Hong Kong is very expensive

While Hong Kong has a reputation for being an expensive city, it's possible to find affordable options for dining, shopping, and entertainment. There are plenty of budget-friendly restaurants, street markets, and free or low-cost attractions to explore.

Hong Kong's culture is just a mix of British and Chinese influences

Although the city has been shaped by both British and Chinese influences due to its colonial past, Hong Kong's culture is unique and cannot be solely defined by these two elements. The city has a distinctive identity that has been shaped by various regional and global influences.

Hong Kong is always crowded

While some areas of Hong Kong are densely populated, there are quieter neighbourhoods and green spaces where you can escape the hustle and bustle. Exploring the outlying islands, beaches, and country parks can provide a peaceful retreat from the city's busy streets.

Hong Kong lacks political freedom

The political situation in Hong Kong is complex, and the relationship with mainland China has raised concerns about political freedom in recent years. However, it's important to recognize that Hong Kong maintains a separate legal system and enjoys a degree of autonomy under the "one country, two systems" principle.

People in Hong Kong are unfriendly or rude

Visitors to Hong Kong may perceive the locals as unfriendly or rude, but this is often a misunderstanding of cultural differences. People in Hong Kong tend to be more reserved and may not engage in small talk with strangers, but they are generally helpful and respectful when approached for assistance.

Strategies for overcoming biases and promoting understanding

Promoting understanding and overcoming biases is essential for fostering a more inclusive and harmonious society. Here are some strategies to help overcome biases and promote understanding among individuals from different backgrounds and cultures:

Educate yourself

Learn about different cultures, religions, and traditions to better understand the perspectives and experiences of others. Read books, attend workshops, or take courses to deepen your knowledge and appreciation of different cultural backgrounds.

Engage in open dialogue

Engage in open and respectful conversations with people from diverse backgrounds. Ask questions, listen actively, and share your own experiences to foster mutual understanding and respect.

Challenge stereotypes and assumptions

Be aware of your own biases and challenge any stereotypes or assumptions you may hold about people from different cultures. Recognize that individuals are unique and cannot be defined solely by their cultural or ethnic background.

Practice empathy

Put yourself in others' shoes and try to understand their feelings, perspectives, and experiences. Empathy helps create a deeper connection and fosters mutual understanding and respect.

Be open-minded

Approach new experiences and ideas with curiosity and an open mind. Be willing to learn from others and embrace the diversity of perspectives and experiences they bring.

Encourage cultural exchange

Organize or participate in cultural exchange activities, such as international food nights, language exchange groups, or cultural performances. These events provide opportunities for people to share and learn about each other's cultures and traditions.

Create inclusive environments

Foster inclusive environments in your workplace, school, or community by promoting diversity and inclusion policies, celebrating multicultural events, and encouraging open dialogue and collaboration among diverse groups.

Address discrimination and prejudice

Speak up against discrimination and prejudice when you witness it, and support policies and initiatives that promote equality and social justice.

Be a role model

Set an example for others by demonstrating respect, open-mindedness, and empathy in your interactions with people from different cultural backgrounds. Encourage others to do the same and work together to promote understanding and inclusivity.

Reflect on your own biases

Regularly reflect on your own biases and prejudices and make a conscious effort to challenge them. Recognize that overcoming biases is an ongoing process that requires self-awareness, humility, and a commitment to growth and learning.

13. BUILDING CROSS-CULTURAL RELATIONSHIPS

Effective Communication and Conflict Resolution

Effective communication and conflict resolution are key components of building cross-cultural relationships. Here are some tips for expats on effective communication and conflict resolution:

Learn the language

Learning some basic phrases can help you communicate more effectively with the local community. This can help you establish rapport and build relationships.

Be aware of nonverbal cues

Be aware of nonverbal cues such as body language and tone of voice, which can vary depending on the culture. Locals may use indirect communication and nonverbal cues to express their thoughts and feelings, so it's important to be sensitive to these cues.

Listen actively

Active listening is an important part of effective communication. Take the time to listen to the perspectives and concerns and show that you understand and value their opinions.

Be respectful

Be respectful of the culture and traditions. Show interest and respect for their beliefs and customs and avoid imposing your own values or beliefs.

Avoid confrontation

Locals may avoid confrontation or direct conflict, preferring instead to use indirect communication and negotiation. Be mindful of this and avoid being confrontational in your communication style.

Seek to understand

Seek to understand the perspective and context in any conflict or disagreement. This can help you find common ground and work towards a mutually acceptable solution.

Be patient

Building cross-cultural relationships takes time and patience. Be patient in your communication and conflict resolution and be willing to compromise and find creative solutions.

Adapting to cultural differences

Adapting to cultural differences is an important part of living as an expat. Here are some tips for expats on how to adapt to cultural differences:

Learn about the culture

Learn about the culture and customs before you arrive. This can help you understand the social norms, values, and beliefs.

Respect local customs

Respect local customs and traditions, even if they are different from what you are used to. Show interest in the culture and be willing to learn and adapt.

Develop relationships

Develop relationships, whether it's with colleagues, neighbours, or friends. This can help you gain a better understanding of the culture and develop a support network.

Learn the language

Learning some basic phrases can help you communicate more effectively and show that you respect their culture.

Be patient

Be patient and understanding of cultural differences. Locals may have a different sense of time, communication style, and decision-making process than what you are used to.

Be flexible

Be flexible and adaptable in your approach to work and socializing. Residents may have different work and social customs, so be willing to adjust your expectations and approach.

Embrace new experiences

Embrace new experiences and try new things, such as trying local food, attending cultural events, or visiting new places. This can help you appreciate and enjoy the unique aspects of the culture.

Developing empathy and cultural intelligence

Developing empathy and cultural intelligence is essential for fostering meaningful cross-cultural relationships, both personally and professionally. In this chapter, we will discuss strategies and tips for cultivating empathy and cultural intelligence to better connect with people from different backgrounds.

Educate yourself about different cultures.

Invest time in learning about the values, customs, and traditions of various cultures, especially those you frequently interact with. Understanding cultural nuances can help you appreciate their perspectives and anticipate potential communication challenges.

Engage in active listening.

Make a conscious effort to listen attentively to others, without interrupting or imposing your own opinions. Active listening can help you gain deeper insights into their experiences, feelings, and perspectives, which is crucial for developing empathy.

Practice perspective-taking.

Put yourself in the shoes of others and try to understand their thoughts, emotions, and experiences from their point of view. This can help you appreciate the challenges they face and foster empathy and understanding.

Develop emotional intelligence.

Emotional intelligence refers to the ability to recognize, understand, and manage your own emotions and the emotions of others. Enhancing your emotional intelligence can help you better understand the emotional underpinnings of cross-cultural interactions and respond more empathetically.

Be curious and open-minded.

Approach cultural differences with curiosity and an open mind. Ask questions and seek to learn more about the experiences and perspectives of others, without judgment or preconceived notions.

Observe and reflect on cultural interactions.

Pay close attention to how you and others respond to cultural differences in various contexts. Reflect on these interactions to identify areas where you can improve your empathy and cultural intelligence.

Seek diverse experiences and relationships.

Expose yourself to diverse experiences and relationships by interacting with people from different cultural backgrounds. These experiences can help you develop a broader understanding of the world and enhance your empathy and cultural intelligence.

Foster a growth mindset.

Embrace a growth mindset, which involves viewing challenges as opportunities for learning and growth. This mindset can help you approach cultural differences with a willingness to learn and adapt, rather than feeling threatened or overwhelmed.

Participate in cultural training and workshops.

Consider attending workshops or participating in cultural training programs to enhance your understanding of different cultures and develop your empathy and cultural intelligence.

Continuously learn and adapt.

Recognize that developing empathy and cultural intelligence is an ongoing process that requires continuous learning, reflection, and adaptation. Stay committed to personal growth and be open to feedback and new experiences.

14. CASE STUDIES AND REAL LIFE EXAMPLES

Stories and anecdotes illustrating cultural challenges and successes

These stories and anecdotes illustrate the importance of understanding, adapting to, and embracing cultural differences in order to overcome challenges and achieve success in multicultural environments. By being open-minded, respectful, and curious about other cultures, individuals can foster greater understanding, mutual respect, and successful collaboration across cultural boundaries.

Adapting to Different Communication Styles:

A British expat working in Hong Kong found it challenging to adapt to the local communication style, which is often more indirect and subtle compared to the more straightforward communication style she was used to in the UK. Over time, she learned to read between the lines and pay more attention to nonverbal cues and context. This helped her develop better relationships with her colleagues and clients in Hong Kong, as she was able to understand their needs and expectations more effectively.

Overcoming Language Barriers:

A Canadian couple moved to Hong Kong and initially struggled with the language barrier, as they only spoke English and French. They decided to enrol in Cantonese classes to learn the local language and found that their efforts to learn Cantonese greatly improved their experience in Hong Kong. They were able to communicate more effectively with local residents, navigate the city with greater ease, and gain a deeper understanding of Hong Kong's culture and traditions.

Embracing Cultural Differences:

An Indian software engineer relocated to Hong Kong for work and found the local food culture to be quite different from what he was used to back home. Instead of sticking to familiar Indian dishes, he decided to embrace the local cuisine and try new foods. He discovered that he enjoyed many traditional Cantonese dishes, and his willingness to try new foods helped him bond with his local co-workers and neighbours, leading to a more enriching experience in his new home.

Celebrating Cultural Diversity:

A multinational company based in Hong Kong organized a multicultural festival for its employees, encouraging them to share their native cuisine, traditional dress, and cultural performances. This event helped to break down cultural barriers among employees from diverse backgrounds, fostering greater understanding, and appreciation for each other's cultures. The event not only boosted morale but also facilitated better collaboration and teamwork among the employees.

Lessons learned and best practices

From the stories and anecdotes illustrating cultural challenges and successes, we can derive several key lessons and best practices for navigating multicultural environments:

Be aware of cultural nuances

Understand that communication styles, body language, and social norms can vary significantly across cultures. Be observant and attentive to these nuances to avoid misunderstandings and foster better communication.

Learn the local language

Even a basic understanding of the local language can greatly improve your ability to communicate and connect with people from different cultural backgrounds. It shows your respect for their culture and helps you navigate daily life more easily.

Be open to new experiences

Embrace the opportunity to learn about and experience different cultures, traditions, and cuisines. This will not only enrich your personal growth but also enable you to build stronger relationships with people from diverse backgrounds.

Practice empathy and active listening

Try to put yourself in others' shoes and listen to their perspectives and experiences without judgment. Empathy and active listening are crucial for fostering mutual understanding and respect.

Adapt your communication style

Be aware of your own communication style and be willing to adapt it to the cultural context you are in. This may involve being more direct or indirect, depending on the situation and the cultural norms of the people you are interacting with.

Foster inclusivity and celebrate diversity

Create inclusive environments in your workplace, school, or community by promoting diversity and inclusion policies, celebrating multicultural events, and encouraging open dialogue and collaboration among diverse groups.

Address discrimination and prejudice

Speak up against discrimination and prejudice when you witness it and support policies and initiatives that promote equality and social justice.

Engage in cultural exchange

Participate in or organize cultural exchange activities to promote understanding and appreciation of different cultures and traditions. These events provide opportunities for people to share and learn about each other's cultures.

Be a role model

Set an example for others by demonstrating respect, open-mindedness, and empathy in your interactions with people from different cultural backgrounds. Encourage others to do the same and work together to promote understanding and inclusivity.

Reflect on your own biases

Regularly reflect on your own biases and prejudices and make a conscious effort to challenge them. Recognize that overcoming biases is an ongoing process that requires self-awareness, humility, and a commitment to growth and learning.

Resources and Further Reading

Books, articles, and websites for further exploration

Books:

- "Gweilo: Memories of a Hong Kong Childhood" by Martin Booth - An autobiographical account of the author's childhood in post-war Hong Kong, providing a glimpse into the city's history and culture.
- "Hong Kong: Culture Smart! The Essential Guide to Customs & Culture" by Clare Vickers - A practical guide to understanding Hong Kong's culture, customs, and traditions.
- "City of Protest: A Recent History of Dissent in Hong Kong" by Antony Dapiran - A book that explores the city's tradition of protest and the struggle for democracy in the context of its complex relationship with mainland China.
- "Fragrant Harbour" by John Lanchester - A historical novel set in Hong Kong, spanning different periods in the city's history from the 1930s to the 1990s.

Articles:

- **"Hong Kong's History: From Backwater to Metropolis"** by Tony Banham - This article offers an overview of Hong Kong's history, from its early days as a small fishing village to its present-day status as a global financial centre.
- **"Understanding Hong Kong's Culture"** by Jason Wordie - An article that provides insights into the unique cultural identity of Hong Kong, influenced by both Chinese and British traditions.

Websites & Blogs:

- **Hofstede Insights** (https://www.hofstede-insights.com/) - This website offers tools and resources for understanding and comparing national cultural dimensions based on Geert Hofstede's research.
- **The Culture Trip** (https://theculturetrip.com/) - A website featuring articles and stories about different cultures, travel, and local experiences around the world.
- **World Business Culture** (https://www.worldbusinessculture.com/) - This website provides country-specific information on business culture, etiquette, and practices.
- **Intercultural Communication Institute** (https://intercultural.org/) - The Institute offers resources, training, and conferences on intercultural communication and competence.
- **Living Language** (https://www.livinglanguage.com/) - A language learning platform that also offers insights into different cultures and customs.

Language learning resources and cultural organisations

Language Learning Resources:

- **Hong Kong Tourism Board** (https://www.discoverhongkong.com/) - The official website for Hong Kong tourism, offering information on attractions, events, and local culture.
- **Hong Kong Heritage Project** (https://www.hongkongheritage.org/) - A website dedicated to preserving and sharing Hong Kong's unique cultural heritage, featuring oral histories, photographs, and historical documents.
- **Time Out Hong Kong** (https://www.timeout.com/hong-kong) - An online city guide that covers the latest news on Hong Kong's arts, culture, dining, and entertainment scenes.
- **Hong Kong Free Press** (https://hongkongfp.com/) - An independent, non-profit news outlet that provides coverage of Hong Kong's politics, society, and culture.

- **Asia Society Hong Kong Center** (https://asiasociety.org/hong-kong) - A leading educational organization dedicated to fostering a deeper understanding of Asia, offering a diverse array of programs in arts, culture, education, and policy.

- **Hong Kong Arts Centre** (https://www.hkac.org.hk/) - A non-profit organization promoting contemporary arts and culture through exhibitions, performances, film screenings, and educational events.

- **Hong Kong Heritage Museum** (https://www.heritagemuseum.gov.hk/) - A museum dedicated to preserving and promoting Hong Kong's history, art, and culture, offering exhibitions, educational programs, and events.

- **Hong Kong Cultural Centre** (https://www.lcsd.gov.hk/CE/CulturalService/HKCC/en/index.php) - A major venue for cultural events, including music, dance, and theatre performances, operated by the Leisure and Cultural Services Department of the Hong Kong government.

- **Hong Kong Museum of History** (https://hk.history.museum/) - This museum showcases the history, culture, and natural environment of Hong Kong through exhibitions, educational programs, and events.

- **Hong Kong Film Archive** (https://www.lcsd.gov.hk/CE/CulturalService/HKFA/en_US/web/hkfa/home.html) - A government-run institution dedicated to the preservation and promotion of Hong Kong's film heritage, offering screenings, exhibitions, and publications.

www.ingramcontent.com/pod-product-compliance
Lightning Source LLC
Chambersburg PA
CBHW070456220526
45466CB00004B/1852